Church Planting

in the

African-American Community

CHURCH PLANTING
IN THE
AFRICAN-AMERICAN COMMUNITY

JOE S. RATLIFF AND MICHAEL J. COX

BROADMAN PRESS
NASHVILLE, TENNESSEE

© Copyright 1993 • Broadman Press
All Rights Reserved

4260-71

ISBN: 0-8054-6071-3

Dewey Decimal Classification: 254.1
Subject Heading: New Churches // Church Planting // Black Churches
Library of Congress Card Catalog Number: 92-31305
Printed in the United States of America

Unless otherwise stated, all Scripture quotations are
from the *King James Version of the Bible.*

Scripture quotations marked NASB are from the
New American Standard Bible. © The Lockman Foundation,
1960, 1962, 1963, 1968, 1971, 1972, 1973, 1975, 1977.
Used by permission.

Library of Congress Cataloging-in-Publication Data

Ratliff, Joe S., 1950-
    Church planting in the African–American community / Joe S.
Ratliff and Michael J. Cox.
        p.   cm.
    Includes bibliographical references.
    ISBN: 0-8054-6071-3
    1. Afro-Americans—Mission. 2. Church development, New—
Baptists. 3. Southern Baptist Convention—Missions. 4. Southern
Baptist Convention—Membership. 5. Afro-American Baptists.
I. Cox, Michael J., 1957-   II. Title.
BV2783.R35 1993
254'.1'08996073—dc20   92-31305
                                                                CIP

Acknowledgments

We wish to express our love and appreciation to our loving wives, son and godson Michael Phillip Cox, and Brentwood Baptist Church in Houston, Texas. They have continued to provide encouragement and inspiration in our journey to start churches in black communities across the nation.

A special word of thanks is given for the valuable assistance of Margaret Dempsey, Kathleen Curate, Vicki Jones, and Deborah Jordan. They provided expert professional guidance in the writing of this book.

90648

Contents

Foreword

Fifteen years ago I began to think seriously about the issues and problems related to starting churches in America's predominantly black communities. When I talked about that interest, my friends, both black and white, said, "No new churches are needed in black communities. Sometimes there are three storefront Missionary Baptist churches in one city block in the inner city!"

Their observations about the number and proximity of black Baptist churches are, of course, correct. This fact stimulated a question in my mind. How did we get all these black churches in the inner cities of our nation?

My research uncovered what I believe is the greatest untold church-planting story of the twentieth century. In 1900 there were a few black churches in Northern industrial cities. Today there are thousands. This growth has mainly taken place without planning, without outside support, and without human supervision. It was done at great sacrifice by church planter-pastors who made their own living. Their achievements have been enormous, and continue as new black communities develop and as established black communities change.

However, that paradigm is now shifting. Church planting in black communities is becoming more intentional. Strong black churches are deliberately, under the Holy Spirit's leadership, training and sending out church planters. Pastors of predominantly black churches are supervising these church planters. Monetary support is coming from these sponsoring churches.

This book is the first serious effort to get at the nuts and bolts of this process. It is written by two men with experience in intentional church planting. Joe Ratliff is a genuine scholar-pastor with the heart of an evangelist. His church, Brentwood Baptist of Houston, has more than five thousand in Sunday worship and has an intensive, intentional commitment to multiplying new congregations. Michael Cox has served as minister of youth in that church. Further, he has planted a strong church on the new paradigm and has been part of a national denominational team involved in church extension in predominantly black communities. He is a young man marked for leadership in this era at the turning of the millenium.

Who should read this book? Everyone interested in church growth, church planting, and evangelism; everyone interested in reaching the great cities of America; leaders of denominational programs committed to church extension or new church development; leaders of predominantly black churches; leaders of churches in transitional communities; mission professors; seminarians; all who love the Lord Jesus Christ and want to see the lost found; and those who care about impacting the moral culture of this nation with Judeo-Christian values. Especially those who believe God is calling them to plant a church in a predominantly black community.

Foreword

Although written from a Southern Baptist perspective, this book can be translated into any denominational language. I highly commend it.

Charles L. Chaney
Vice-President, Home Mission Board, Extension

1

Jesus' Journey/
Our Journey

Let us embark on a journey. This journey will not be a restful vacation at a mountaintop resort or even a Sunday afternoon drive down an idyllic country road.

Rather, it will be a difficult journey—one with various curves in the road and turbulence in the skies. It will be a long journey—one that, once we have started, we may often wonder, "When are we going to get there?" or even "Are we there yet?"

We may be tempted to ask, "Why should we make this journey if it is so arduous and seemingly unending?" We make this journey because it is necessary. It is one of those trips that we know we must make, but if given a choice, we would just as soon not go.

Jesus' Necessary Journey

Jesus is our model in making this necessary, but difficult, journey. In John 4, we read the familiar story of Jesus and His encounter with the Samaritan woman. In interpreting this passage, we often focus on the ensuing relationship that developed between Jesus and the woman, rather than on the journey that brought Jesus there.

Consider the journey.[1] John describes the journey as necessary for Jesus, "he must needs go through Samaria"

(v. 4). Although Samaria was the direct path from Judea to Galilee, most devout Jews did not take this way. Because of the hatred and contempt that the Jews held for the Samaritans—the half-breeds—they went out of their way to avoid them, even if such avoidance meant numerous inconveniences. But Jesus, however, had no choice. It was necessary for Him to take the direct path, to go through rather than around Samaria.

This necessary journey for Jesus was rife with difficulties. First, the journey was historically unprecedented. The Jews had set a historic precedent for going around Samaria. Jesus shocked the religious establishment by ignoring history. He chose to make some history of His own.

Second, the journey was culturally unacceptable. Culturally, the two groups did not mix. The Jews saw the Samaritan culture as an abomination of what God intended for the Jews to be. The cultural dichotomy between the two groups was offensive to the Jews.

Third, the journey was theologically unsound. The Jews, God's chosen ones, were completely intolerant of Samaritans. The Jews had religious reasons to back them up. Surely God would agree with them that, because the Samaritans had corrupted their racial purity and had turned to pagan influences, they deserved no contact with God's elect. Rightfully, they were to be ignored and, at least peripherally, forgotten.

Fourth, the journey was politically inexpedient. In Jesus' day, political and religious leaders were so intertwined that to offend one was to offend the other. Jesus risked offending not only the religious leaders but also the political authorities with His journey.

Fifth, the journey was economically unfeasible. Jesus relied on the generosity and goodness of others to care for

His most basic needs. Here, He was entering into "enemy territory." He would not be welcome. He might not be cared for. He certainly would not be indulged. More than likely He would leave that place with nothing more than what He went into it with, possibly with less.

Sixth, the journey was socially unacceptable. Crossing through Samaria meant that, somewhere along the journey, the traveler would have to come into contact with the hated Samaritans. The Jews could think of no group of people whom they abhorred more than the Samaritans. Even the thought of having any social contact with the Samaritans was repulsive to the Jews.

Against these odds—historical, cultural, theological, political, economic, social—and perhaps others, Jesus set out on His journey. Despite the difficulties, Jesus accomplished what He set out to do. He was able to share the riches of His Father with one who was despised by others. Was Jesus trying to make some kind of statement with His journey? If anything, His statement would be that the gospel is for all, not just for the elect, the rich, the beautiful, the white, the pure, the lovable—the list could go on interminably. The point is clear.

The gospel is for all.

Our Necessary Journey

That same conviction drives us on our journey today. This particular journey as Southern Baptists, simply put, is to start churches in predominantly black communities. The journey sounds simple, but consider the odds.

First, such a journey seems to put us at odds with our history as Southern Baptists. The Southern Baptist Convention at its inception in 1845 was openly proslavery and segregationist. Despite this stance, Southern Baptists succumbed to the belief that blacks had souls and were capable of being saved—if "they" stayed comfortably and innocuously in "their" churches. Is this the same denomination that today is launching an aggressive campaign to start churches in black communities?

Second, such a journey seems to put us at odds with reigning culture. Although blacks and whites are at least theoretically treated as equals, a quiet racism threatens to rock us into a numbing complacency. Consider the facts: African-American men comprise 6 percent of the American population, 3.5 percent of our nation's college enrollment, and a startling 46 percent of our nation's prison population.[2] Further, 33 percent of blacks in America, as compared to 9 percent of whites in America, live below the poverty level.[3] Other statistics could be given. Racial equality seems to be the exception rather than the norm. Is this culture ready for a predominantly white denomination to enter predominantly black communities to start churches?

Third, such a journey seems to put us at odds with popular theology. Despite all of our theoretical protests to the contrary, popular theology does not seem to practically embrace the heterogeneous-unit principle. Eleven o'clock on Sunday morning is still the most segregated hour during the week. Keep in mind that we are proposing starting churches in predominantly black communities, not black churches. There is a difference, however subtle. Is our theology open enough to sometimes forego what has defensively been called human nature to follow God's nature?

Fourth, such a journey seems to put us at odds with contemporary political maneuverings. As blacks, who have long been politically downtrodden, become a national force to be reckoned with, the call for "common ground" becomes a cheer for one-race tickets. If you vote for the "race" of your choice, you are promised that you will be the beneficiary. Such jockeying for political power and position contradicts Southern Baptists' vocal commitment to justice. Is the political establishment far enough removed from our religious world that the two shall never meet, or does there need to be more acting and less talking from both the religious and political worlds about "liberty and justice for all"?

Fifth, such a journey seems economically unfeasible. In this final decade of the twentieth century, the bottom line is what counts. With an accountant-type accuracy, we can calculate the relative success or failure of any venture— even church starting. To start churches in black communities means that some will never be successful by twentieth-century standards. Some of these churches must be started in ghettos or in housing projects. These churches will never be self-supporting; they may never be large. Are we ready to put away the tally sheets and announce that "Whatever the cost, we are willing"?

Sixth, such a journey seems to put us at odds with socially acceptable behavior. Once again, a quiet racism invades our thinking. Southern Baptists have often been accused of paternalism. Many see Southern Baptists holding out the carrots of financial and resource assistance to struggling black churches. Traditional black churches have been accused, through no fault of their own, of not having the resources to do what must be done to reach America's black population for Christ. Are Southern Baptists and other traditional black denominations willing to quit bickering and make it socially acceptable for blacks and whites to work together to reach the unreached, whatever their race?

The odds seem to be against us. But, with the conviction that what we are doing is inspired of God, the odds are surmountable.

That's what this book is about—overcoming the odds. It's about doing the impossible and sometimes the unpopular.

The Southern Baptist Convention currently has approximately fifteen hundred churches in predominantly black communities. The goal is to have five thousand churches in predominantly black communities by the year 2000. That's more than a 200 percent increase in the number of churches in black communities in less than ten years. In close to one hundred fifty years, Southern Baptists can count fifteen hundred churches in black communities. And, we want to more than double that number by the year 2000! Sounds impossible.

As Southern Baptists attempt to reach the unreached black and start 3,500 churches by the year 2000, we cannot assume that others are sitting idly by, applauding our efforts. The opposite is true. Southern Baptists' reaching into black communities has been described by outsiders as "poaching on souls." Sounds unpopular.

This book answers the "why" and the "how" of reaching this outwardly impossible, and often unpopular, goal. The purpose of this book is to present a theology and strategy for church planting and growth in the black community.

Notice the little article "a" in that purpose statement. This book purports nothing more, nothing less than to present *a* theology and strategy. It would be folly to attempt to present *the* theology and strategy. Without trying to downplay the conviction that the writers of this book have regarding their theology and strategy, it must be recognized that situations, and thus strategies, vary and that people's perception of theology mature, change, and evolve. Much of the theology and strategy presented here unapologetically comes as a direct result of the church-starting experiences of the writers and of their "growing up in the Southern Baptist Convention." Accept this book in its purest intentions—a theology and strategy.

Rationale

Why do we need a theology and strategy for church planting and growth in the black community? Several reasons are evident.

Lack of Intentionality in Church Starting

In the past, church starting in black communities lacked intentionality. Churches seemed to appear, and sometimes disappear, overnight. There is a plausible explanation for why church planting and growth in black communities has so long been on the back burner.

Historically, the church for black people was an "all in all." The black church helped to define and defend black culture. The black church provided a sense of equality and dignity to those who were downtrodden in everyday living. Perhaps the most important gift that the historical black church offered its constituents was a "theology of hope," not only for the hereafter, but also for day-to-day living.

Because of the centrality of the church in black people's lives, its existence and propagation were natural. There was no question that where the people were, the church would be there also, in one form or another. The church just "happened." Church starting was informal and sometimes spontaneous. If a new church was needed, it was started. These churches were started and grown with as little interference from whites as possible.

Through the years, the role of the church in the black community has changed. No longer is it the all in all. While the black church still offers a theology of hope, blacks have other avenues in which to work for justice, to build family, to be entertained, to learn. Thus, the church is not as much a natural outgrowth of people's lives as it was in the past. The church doesn't just happen; it must be made to happen. To meet today's challenges and needs for churches in black communities, we must deliberately and prayerfully seek locations, invest resources, and persevere until a congregation is begun.

Number of Unchurched Blacks

The second reason why a theology and strategy for church planting and growth in black communities is desperately needed is related to the first reason. A large number of blacks are what researchers label "unchurched." In March 1988 the Gallup organization conducted a national religious survey of the adult population in America. According to this study, 40 percent of all blacks in America are unchurched. The unchurched in this survey were defined in three ways: (1) church members who have not attended church within the past six months, (2) nonchurch members who have attended church within the past six months, and (3) nonchurch members who have not attended church within the past six months. It must be noted that the percentage of unchurched blacks does not differ significantly from the percentages of unchurched whites (44 percent) and Hispanics (45 percent).

Interestingly, 86 percent of all surveyed blacks indicated that religion was at least "fairly important" to them. This includes 69 percent of the unchurched blacks. In response to a question directed specifically to the unchurched, who at one time had been more active in church than they are presently, 73 percent of blacks indicated a possibility that they would become "fairly active members of a church or synagogue." These statistics seem to imply that something may be missing from existing blacks churches. It also seems to indicate that a high number of unchurched blacks would be good prospects for church membership.

The next question becomes, "Why are the unchurched unchurched?" Reasons are varied and many. However, one fairly reliable indicator has to do with attitude toward organized religion. Here, racial delineations show more variations. Fifty-one percent of blacks, as compared to 40 percent of both whites and Hispanics, are concerned about what they consider to be the churches' insufficient concern with social-justice issues. Further, 70 percent of blacks agree that "one church is as good as another," as compared to 60 percent of Hispanics, and 54 percent of whites. While attitude toward organized religion is not the only indicator for why people do not attend, it is a fairly accurate barometer of "where people are."

Lack of Resources on the Topic

A third reason why a theology and strategy for church planting and growth in the black community is a desperate need is because of a conspicuous lack of written resources on the topic. A bibliography of resources related to religion in black America is included on page 101 of this book. These resources are commendable and insightful. However, even a cursory scan of these resources indicates a dearth of information on church planting and growth in the black community.

The lack of such resources is certainly not an oversight. It is a testimony to the place that church planting and growth have been relegated in the black community. Church planting and growth in the black community have not been priorities; now, they must be.

Other reasons for articulating a strategy and theology for church planting and growth in the black community can be stated. However, for the purpose of this book, these reasons seem to be the most overarching and pertinent.

Target Audience

The target audience of this book is you. Whether you are a black or white pastor of a Southern Baptist or National Baptist church; a Southern Baptist Convention, state, or associational leader; a seminary student or professor; a leader from the American Baptist Convention; or a layperson, this book is for you. The target audience of this book has intentionally been kept as wide and as open as possible. The reason for that is simple. Church planting and growth in black communities do not belong to any one group. Enough lost people live in these communities for everyone to be concerned. It would be arrogant for any group to pretend that they "owned" or had exclusive rights to evangelize those lost people based upon the color of their skin. We must all be concerned and active in reaching into these black communities and sharing Christ with the residents.

Because the audience is so broad, few generalizations can be made. However, at least one assumption is made about the book's readers. That is if you are reading this book, you are at least nominally interested in church planting in black communities. Now that interest may be influenced by any number of factors—such as credit in a class or just plain curiosity. Whatever the influence, the interest is there. The authors hope to take that interest and give it some information with which to grow.

Contents

Because this book presents an overall theology and strategy for church planting in the black community, it is organized topically, not chronologically or sequentially as in a how-to book. In selecting and discussing topics, the authors tried to consider and answer various questions that would be asked by people interested in starting and growing churches in black communities.

Chapter 2 examines nine church starts in which the authors were directly involved. What lessons do these church starts offer to the church willing to start a new church? To the new church wanting to become established?

Chapter 3 speaks to the matter of taking your interest or vision for church planting in the black community and translating it into action. Why would anyone want to start churches in black communities in the 1990s? How can one determine if there is really a need for a new church in a particular community? How can various people, such as a sponsoring pastor, director of missions, church planter, church members, be inspired to buy into the vision and need for a new church?

Chapter 4 presents an understanding of the role of the church sponsor. What types of churches would make appropriate sponsors for churches in black communities? Where can these church sponsors be found? How is the relationship between the sponsoring church and new church developed? What responsibilities does the church

sponsor have to accept? When does the relationship between the church sponsor and new church end?

Chapter 5 presents an understanding of the church
planter. What motivates a church planter? What keeps a
church planter on the job when he must face low church
budget, low salary, low attendance, low visibility? What
role does the church planter fulfill in the new congregation? What kind of commitment must the pastor make to
the new congregation?

Chapter 6 identifies several common pitfalls to avoid in
starting churches in black communities. Is the new congregation playing the numbers game? Is the new congregation looking out for number one? How does the new
congregation make decisions? Where does the new congregation fit into the big picture? Is the new congregation
"rehearsing" or "reversing"? Is the new congregation
"standing its ground"? Is the new congregation thinking
about tomorrow? Is the new congregation trying to go it
alone?

How to Use This Book

The information in this book, it is hoped, will help the
person truly interested in starting and growing churches
in black communities. However, there is something that is
significantly more important than any information presented here. That is how the reader uses the information.

Obviously, this is not a coffee table book, intended to
look inviting and be entertaining. This is a book intended
to spur its readers into action. Consider the following
ideas for making the most of it.

Read the book thoughtfully. Take your time. If you're
going to spend time to read a book, then spend the time
wisely. Try to keep distractions to a minimum as you read.

Hold a pen in your hand as you're reading. Underline anything that makes you think, that makes you nod your head in agreement, or that makes you angry. Jot down notes or questions in the margins.

Read the footnotes. Some quotes or thoughts borrowed from others will intrigue you. Find the sources. Read the quotes or thoughts in context.

Read the bibliography. It was not put in the book just to fill blank pages. These books come from a variety of authors and publishers. They speak to a variety of topics. They represent the best in the field. Select a few to read and add to your library.

Talk to others. As you are reading or even after you read the book, talk to others about what you've read. Flip back through the book; notice the underlines or questions. Share those "ahas" or questions with those whom you respect. Ask their opinions and insights.

Do something. After reading the book, make an intentional decision to do something about what you've read. Don't put the book aside and forget about it. Decide to act on it. Your decision might be as simple as giving the book to somebody else to read or as monumental as leading your church to sponsor a church in a black community. It doesn't matter what the act, as long as there is some positive action.

Conclusion

We are preparing for our journey in church planting in black communities. We are packing our bags and buckling our seat belts. The journey will not end with the last page of this book. In fact, that is when the journey truly begins. Where will it take us?

Notes

1. The basic outline describing Jesus' journey through Samaria comes from an address given by Otis Moss Jr., pastor of Olivet Institutional Baptist Church, Cleveland, Ohio, at Emory University, Atlanta, Georgia, September 18, 1990.

2. Gayraud Wilmore, ed., *Black Men in Prison* (Atlanta: ITC Press, 1990), 6.

3. H. Malcolm Newton, *Can the Black Family Be Saved?* (Monterrey, Calif.: African-American Evangelical Press, 1988), 44.

2

Learning from Our Partners in the Faith

The journey continues. Along the way we will experience indescribable joys and heartaches. We will have Sundays that we wish could go on forever and Sundays that we would just as soon forget.

Such are the ups and downs, twists and turns of our journey. As we journey through each of these experiences we are reminded that many have gone before us, allowing their faith to take them to worlds unknown. Their faith has taken them to black communities where others have not dared to go. Their faith has led them to start churches, when the odds were against them.

These forebears become our teachers. They serve as our inspiration. They cheer us on. They help to light our way at its darkest moments. And, when the light reappears, they are there with us, uttering a prayer of thanksgiving.

At times they shout at us; at times they whisper. Yet the message is the same. "It can be done!"

Following a short historic introduction, this chapter will examine nine church starts in black communities in which the two authors were directly related.

Eight of the church starts are located in the Houston, Texas, metropolitan area. Each of these churches was sponsored, at least in part, by Brentwood Baptist Church.

Brentwood, the largest black church in the Southern Baptist Convention, welcomes approximately five thousand upper middle-class people to its services each Sunday morning. Joe Ratliff has served as pastor of Brentwood since 1980.

The other church start, in Euclid, Ohio, was led by Michael Cox, who served as the first black church-planter apprentice of the Home Mission Board from 1987 to 1989.

Zion Baptist Church, Marietta, Georgia

The date is June 10, 1836. The place is First Baptist Church, Marietta, Georgia. Thornton Burk, the white First Baptist minister, is overseeing the church in conference. As a last order of business, he gives the prefunctory invitation to receive new members.

Elizabeth Dobbs, wife of white slaveowner David Dobbs, stands and opens the door of the church to present her slave Dicy for membership.

"Reverend Burk, you know my needlewoman Dicy. . . . Dicy was a member of our church in Elbert County, and she wants to become part of our church here. She says she won't feel right . . . with God, that is, till she does."[1]

A debate ensues.

Daughter of one of the county's white pioneering families, Martha Knight Massey, begins, "We never had . . . one . . . before. It's just that we never had . . . one . . . before, and I never went to a church where they had . . . one . . . before."[2]

Church clerk Posey Maddox intones, "Nobody says I have to sit with darkies on a Sunday."[3]

Continuing her plea, Massey says, "It's not even like we know for sure that they got souls . . . like ours?"[4]

After much discussion and dissension, Dicy is admitted

Learning from Our Partners in the Faith

to the church . . . to sit in the gallery. Soon afterwards, her fellow slaves from the Dobbs household, and then from other households, join First Baptist as well.

Thus begins a thirty-year struggle for both black and white members of First Baptist Church, Marietta, Georgia, to define and live "Christianity" rather than the watered-down "churchianity."[5]

For them the struggle meant making wrenching decisions on issues which, until then, had never even been considered. Among them:

- The decision to expand the gallery, described by one slave as a "little butter mold," to accommodate the large number of blacks coming to worship.[6]
- The decision whether to allow a slave to perform a marriage ceremony for "persons of color."[7]
- The decision whether to allow the "colored brethren . . . the privilege of having an African Church to themselves."[8]
- The decision whether to grant a slave preacher a license to preach.[9]

The context for most of their historic decision making was the church conference. Decisions were made, but not easily. "June 19, 1853. There are 1,149,662 Baptists in the United States . . . 65,639 in Georgia. . . . Of that number, 203 of them are feuding in Marietta."[10]

Black and white members of First Baptist Church, Marietta, Georgia, feuded. They grumbled. They showed almost embarrassing humanness. Yet, in spite of it all, God used them.

The date is April 8, 1866. The place is First Baptist Church, Marietta, Georgia. Thornton Burk, the white First Baptist minister, is overseeing the church in conference.

"The Zion Baptist Church is formally organized by Rev. Ephraim B. Rucker—licensed to preach by the First Baptist Church of Marietta."[11] Thus, Zion Baptist Church, a black church with a licensed black preacher, is begun. The church exists to this day.

How does the beginning of Zion Baptist Church compare with the starting of churches in black communities today—almost one hundred fifty years later?

Tragically, there are many similarities. We still see feuding, grumbling, and humanness from those who are "desperate to understand and desperate not to understand."[12] Yet, today we try not to be quite so blatant in showing these unbecoming traits.

Thankfully, there are some differences. The bridge of mutual respect and understanding between blacks and whites has been strengthened. Yet, more bridge-building must be on our Southern Baptist agenda.

Read on for more contemporary church starts in black communities.

First Baptist Greens Bayou, Houston, Texas

Children jumping rope with a carefree abandon, daring each other to go down the slide headfirst, scurrying into a not-so-straight line when the familiar whistle sounds.

Adults grieving over their neighbors who had left the neighborhood, daring to hold worship services when the pews and parking lot remain close to empty, resorting to using day-care receipts to pay their beloved pastor.

Such was the situation of First Baptist Greens Bayou in 1984. "White flight" had forced a significant transition in the traditionally white middle-class community in north Houston. Frightened church members and their resources left their neighborhoods and their church in droves.

Ten to twelve stalwart members and the pastor stayed. Some members even commuted to their church from other neighborhoods. They were determined. They didn't want to lose their Southern Baptist witness in the community that had been their home for so many years.

Yet the church was reeling from the blows. The only thing that seemed to be "working" for the church was its day-care center. The center attracted neighborhood residents while the church apparently could not.

Brentwood heard of First Baptist Greens Bayou's plight. Sometime earlier Brentwood had entered an agreement with Union Baptist Association that the association would inform Brentwood of any church in significant transition and in danger of closing its doors. Brentwood's intent was pure: to ensure that a Southern Baptist witness would remain in the community and that the church facility would not be sold to the "highest bidder."

Acting as much as a consultant as a sponsoring church, Brentwood assisted First Baptist Greens Bayou in assessing its situation and making the transition from being a church in a predominantly white community to one in a predominantly black community. The white pastor knew what was happening to his community and, when the time came, he was willing to step aside and allow others to continue to build the Christian witness he had begun. For three months, two pastors served the church—the original white pastor; the other, a newly recruited black pastor.

In a history-making event, a constitution service was held, commemorating the church changing its leadership and its constituency. The church kept its name and its affiliation with the Southern Baptist Convention. The white pastor moved to another pastorate. The black pastor took the leadership of the church.

With his personality, people skills, and organizational ability, new pastor M. E. Williams canvassed his neighborhood, where most of the people were new residents without a church home, and he told them about First Baptist Greens Bayou. The church under its new black leadership grew from an initial nine members to almost two hundred in its first year and more than a thousand in its fourth year.

End Time Baptist Church, Houston, Texas

It is Sunday morning. People are streaming from every direction; they are heading in the same direction—Brentwood Baptist Church's massive domed sanctuary. A few, however, are not going into the dome. Instead they are entering Brentwood's chapel. Once inside, they smile at one another. They embrace. They have found a home. Their home—End Time Baptist Church, a Brentwood mission.

Begun originally as a Bible study, End Time had a very specific target group—blacks with Caribbean ancestry. The small group began meeting with Brentwood for Sunday morning worship services but soon felt the desire to have a church of its own, a church in which the Caribbean worship style could be enjoyed. Although the people starting End Time were black, they had a different cultural identification than Brentwood's members. Thus, the need for a separate church.

Rather than feeling threatened, Brentwood affirmed End Time's need to have an identity of its own. Brentwood offered the use of its chapel, free of charge, for two years. During that time, 1984 to 1986, the group grew from about twenty to seventy-five people. Brentwood then assisted the congregation in locating and renting a day-care center for its worship services. Although still small numerically, the church continues to grow and in 1989 called a new pastor, Matthew Ogbonmwan.

St. Paul Baptist Church, Houston, Texas

Fried chicken, ham, baked beans, potato salad, congealed salad, chocolate cake. Sounds like a family reunion or the ever-popular dinner-on-the-grounds. In this case, however, it is a kick-off event for a new church, St. Paul Baptist Church.

Begun in 1986 under the joint sponsorship of Brentwood and an Anglo church in north Houston, St. Paul reaches upper middle-class blacks. Many erroneously assume that church starting in the black community necessarily means church starting in a low-income area. St. Paul puts that assumption to rest. St. Paul is located in The Woodlands, a planned community of homes starting at around $200,000, just north of Houston.

Reaching upper-income people, whether black or white, means using different methods than those used in reaching lower-income people. Methods used in reaching people must be based directly on people's felt needs.

In The Woodlands, most of the residents commute daily the approximately thirty miles to Houston to work. Once they are home in the evening, they rarely venture out to socialize or meet neighbors.

The picnic offered community residents an opportunity not only to learn about the new church but also to become acquainted with their neighbors. Advertised through telephone calls, through professionally printed flyers and letters, and by word-of-mouth, the picnic attracted a good group. As a result of the picnic, twelve people began meeting for Bible study at the home of Jimmy Dotson, Houston's deputy chief of police. The congregation soon moved to the community's interfaith center for its "Baptist hour." Other denominations worshiped in that same facility at different hours. In its first year, St. Paul grew to fifty-six people, and currently attracts well over two hundred people to its worship services.

The church has a good economic base because its members' incomes are high and because the congregation saved money while worshiping in the interfaith center. Thus, the congregation has purchased six acres of land on which to build its own facility.

Greenspoint Baptist Church, Houston, Texas

Take a husband/wife seminary-trained team and about ten or so couples from Brentwood. Provide generous start-up funds. Wait about four years. The end result? Greenspoint Baptist Church began in 1986 and excelled to reach a 1991 membership of approximately twelve hundred members.

In north Houston, another community was in racial transition, moving from being predominantly white to being predominantly black. Losing its white constituency, the community maintained its economic stability with the newly arriving blacks.

Union Baptist Association viewed this changing community as an opportunity, rather than as a problem. When Brentwood was approached with the possibility of starting a church in this newly emerging black community, it responded not just with dollars but with people. A sponsoring church's resources often go beyond the routine. Resources include financial as well as people investments. In investing approximately twenty-five of its members to start Greenspoint, Brentwood has reached more than a thousand people that otherwise might not have been reached.

Faith Baptist Church, Houston, Texas

Too often, a church split means only pain and misunderstanding. Yet Faith Baptist Church, which began as a split from another church, moved beyond its pain and misunderstanding. It now is a positive and growing influence for Christ in its community.

Faith began with a handful of members meeting in a hotel for several months. With an emphasis on life-style evangelism, community ministry, and visitation and canvassing, the church soon became too large for its hotel home.

Faith's pastor Alvin Molten, an aggressive self-made man, knew a new facility had to be found. With no Southern Baptist background, Molten still knew of Brentwood's church-starting reputation. Molten approached Brentwood with a plea for assistance. Brentwood leaders had never heard of Molten or Faith Church until Molten called to set up an appointment. Molten's people skills and obvious dream won him a hearing. Brentwood heard Molten's presentation, did necessary research to ascertain the validity of Molten's claims, and agreed to the sponsorship.

One of Brentwood's first tasks as a sponsor was to help Faith find a suitable location for its growing congregation. An Anglo congregation was vacating its facility in the suburbs which soon became the home for Faith. Another significant task for Brentwood has been educating Molten in what it means to be Southern Baptist. Since his first contact with Brentwood, Molten has become a very active contributor to the Baptist association.

Begun in 1987 with thirty-seven people, Faith today boast eleven hundred members, and is still growing.

Bissonnet Baptist Church, Houston Texas

A few miles west of the inner city, a stark warehouse provides a meeting place for Bissonnet Baptist Church, another mission of Brentwood Baptist. Begun in November 1989 as a home Bible study with only thirteen members, the mission now boasts more than four hundred members.

Pastor Steve Crampton, who won the Home Mission Board's church planter of the year award in 1991, says his "spiritual intuition" led him to consider starting a church in this community, a racially transitional neighborhood with no black church. Initial discussions with Union Baptist Association directed Crampton to Brentwood Baptist, where he found assistance in conducting a feasibility study of the area.

Most of the members are in their mid to late thirties. Most seem to be fairly comfortable financially. Others are not. The mission has earmarked 10 percent of each Sunday's offering to help those in need.

Most of the members are black. One active couple, however, is white. The husband, carpenter Dean Taylor, serves as deacon chairman for Bissonnet.

Transforming the warehouse into a church has put Taylor's carpentry skills to the test. He has led work crews to install bathrooms, pews, and seats, and to repair and paint the concrete floor.

Those skills may be further tested if Crampton's plans for the church are fulfilled. Crampton wants to purchase the entire warehouse and renovate it into a school, using adjacent property to build the church facility. And he wants to buy nearby apartments to offer low-income housing to neighborhood residents.

Crampton shares his plans at every opportunity, even in

sermons. "When you realize your reward, you don't have any small plans anymore." Spontaneous clapping emerges from the congregation. They are with him, big plans and all.

Heart of Houston Church, Houston, Texas[14]

On the outskirts of what is known as the "fourth ward," one of Houston's most impoverished, crime-ridden areas, shiny late-model cars turn into the parking lot of Grace Theater, headquarters for a Christian troupe, "The A.D. Players."

The hundred or so who emerge from the cars and make their way toward the theater are casually attired, mostly young, and mostly white. Inside they greet each other warmly, sing Christian choruses accompanied by a guitar, and listen intently as pastor Doug Tipps speaks into a standing microphone.

The theater houses a new church, Heart of Houston Church. Although the atmosphere is casual, the worship service moves like clockwork. It has to. The mission rents the theater by the hour.

Begun just weeks earlier as a home Bible study, this mission is the product of a dream. For ten years, Tipps served as pastor of Houston's River Oaks Baptist Church, a large, wealthy Anglo church. He and his family lived two blocks from a country club and for a while were neighbors of former Texas Governor John Connally.

But Tipps became convinced Southern Baptists were "running from the inner city," leaving entire downtown areas "leavenless." Tipps' dream began to take shape. He wanted to start a church that would welcome people of all races and economic backgrounds, a church that would "address the problems only churches can address." He wanted to start a church that would "recontextualize the gospel," speaking when and where it wasn't expected.

And he didn't want to start a church sponsored by a white, racially homogeneous church. "We would never be able to overcome our parentage," he says.

Tipps found a sponsor in Brentwood church. For Brentwood, sponsorship of Heart of Houston has meant including the pastor and his family on its group insurance plan; helping the church find a suitable location; and offering support, challenge, and encouragement as needed. After finding the necessary sponsorship, Tipps sold his home in the affluent neighborhood, purchased a more modest home, and began the new church.

In addition to intentionally finding a black sponsoring church, Heart of Houston also plans to be intentional in ensuring that church leadership is balanced racially and economically.

Currently, Heart of Houston is reaching middle and upper middle-class people "looking for significance." Many have not attended church in years. They have begun to take hold of Tipps' dream, entering inner-city neighborhoods to hold prayer meetings in the streets, adopting schools, and helping to rebuild families.

Tipps knows building his dream church won't be easy. But he's determined. Heart of Houston, he says, will be "deeply in love with the city."

Southwest Community Baptist Church, Houston, Texas[15]

In a western suburb of Houston, bivocational pastor Gregg Patrick is putting his real estate skills to work in his church. Patrick actively negotiated the purchase of an entire shopping center for Southwest Community Baptist Church to use as its home.

Learning from Our Partners in the Faith

Southwest Community Baptist Church began in 1991 with a nucleus of nineteen people in a home Bible study led by Patrick. Within a year, the church averaged a hundred people in its worship service. Many of the additions have come through Patrick's direct door-to-door witnessing.

The mission currently uses the center unit for worship services and Bible studies. Patrick plans to use the 27,900 square foot complex to house a community center with a Christian academy and day care, cultural arts gallery, Christian book store, musical arts school and gospel music center, and soul-food restaurant. Plans call for building the church's worship center and educational facilities on an adjacent 2.5 acres, which the mission still must buy.

Despite the extensive facility plans, Patrick, who has a National Baptist background, keeps his focus on people. He sees the community center as just one way to reach them.

Many did not understand the need for a new black Southern Baptist church in this quickly developing community, which is only 17 percent black. But Patrick did. To him that 17 percent represents about fifty thousand people, most of whom are in two-career, white-collar families bringing home upper middle-class salaries. Most, according to Patrick, are "unchurched believers." If he has his way, they won't be unchurched for long.

Brentwood's sponsorship of Southwest Community involves very little financial support. Primarily the sponsorship involves a sharing of lay leadership as needed. For example, the Brentwood Woman's Missionary Union director offered assistance in starting a Woman's Missionary Union.

Faith Community Baptist Church, Euclid, Ohio[16]

The community of Euclid, Ohio, just northeast of Cleveland, boasts a population of 72,000, including 5,000 blacks. Two Southern Baptist churches, Willoughby and Mount Calvary (now First Baptist South Euclid) decided their community needed more than one predominantly black church.

To speak to that need, Willoughby members started a bus ministry but soon discovered they were reaching children instead of entire families. "We were trying to find a way to reach black adults because we were only reaching children," says Willoughby pastor Lynton Younger. So the church began a home Bible study and eventually called Michael Cox, a then-recent graduate of Southwestern Baptist Theological Seminary, as church starter.

Cox's first order of business was to determine why two well-intentioned white churches faced such difficulty starting a predominantly black church. The answer—pragmatically understandable but theologically questionable—was simple. People go to church where they feel comfortable, where there are people like them.

When Cox took over the reins of the home Bible study, it had seven members, of which four were white. Within two months, the group had increased to twenty members.

Thus began Faith's struggle to find a suitable location. During its first six months, Faith was forced to relocate three times. The first meeting place beyond the home was an American Baptist church, but the rental agreement lasted only four weeks. While in its American Baptist home, Faith planned a special worship event with a well-known, national figure—Martin Luther King III. Advertised in newspapers and on the radio, that event attracted 120 people but cost Faith its home.

Faith's next location option was Mount Calvary, one of its sponsoring churches. Mount Calvary planned to sell its facilities and merge with another Baptist church. Faith was unable to buy the building, but offered to rent. Instead, Mount Calvary sold its facilities to the nearby black Evangelical Christian Church. So Faith relocated in a local elementary school.

By its first anniversary, Faith could afford to buy or build but could not find a suitable building or land. The church found a vacant lot in the heart of Euclid, but the acreage was zoned for apartments or single-family use. Petitioning the city council to rezone the land for church use, Faith was turned down. The land is now a used car lot.

Despite its many setbacks related to finding a suitable location, Faith survived and grew. The first year for Faith was one of survival, including a period of a spiritual and numerical depression. The second year was marked by spiritual growth—an unplanned, unscheduled revival. Concentrating less on numerical growth and more on leadership and Sunday School, Cox freed the church to begin expecting great things of itself. Faith Community Baptist Church started with faith, survived with faith, and has continued to grow with faith.

For further information on each of these case studies, see appendix A.

Learnings

A cursory examination of the ten church starts presented in this chapter confirms much of what will be extensively discussed in the following chapters of this book. There is much we can learn from them. Consider the following:

Church Planting in the African-American Community

1. *Different methods of outreach reach different people.* The picnic that St. Paul Baptist Church used to introduce its church was target-group specific. Church starters must know the communities in which they want to build churches. They must know the people and their needs. Without such crucial knowledge, church starters would be ill-equipped to use the appropriate outreach methods for their communities.

2. *Location for a new church is critical.* At the same time, Southern Baptists are learning to be creative and flexible in church facilities. In these ten churches alone, facilities included a warehouse, hotel, theater, day-care center, sponsoring church chapel, school, shopping center, and interfaith center. Church starters or sponsors who force a church into a debt-ridden building program too soon pay the price for years to come. Innovative use of already existing buildings generally serves the community as well as the kingdom of God.

3. *Resources are more than money.* While they think most often in terms of money, sponsoring churches have many resources to offer the new church. Some of the resources that Brentwood offered new churches in this chapter included counsel, lay leadership, ministerial leadership, education, facilities, and so forth.

4. *The sponsoring church must have a vision for the kingdom of God rather than for its own somewhat narrow version of "kingdom."* A sponsoring church that is busy guarding its own "turf" has little to offer a new church. Sponsoring churches and new churches must have the attitude that "We're all in this together." While Brentwood Baptist Church "gave" twenty-five of its members to Greenspoint, the kingdom of God gained approximately one thousand people in return.

5. The sponsoring church must accept sponsorship of certain churches with much care and an almost businesslike approach. Because Brentwood Baptist Church did not know Alvin Molten or his church, it approached his request for assistance pragmatically and carefully. A church that actively sponsors one or more new churches will gain a reputation. It will be approached frequently with requests for assistance and/or sponsorship. It is appropriate to hear each request, but not to respond positively to each. Many kind and generous sponsoring churches have felt the pain of betrayal and/or the drain of emotional and financial resources. Sponsoring churches, while open to the Holy Spirit's leadership, must do their homework before agreeing to sponsor a new church.

6. The church starter is an important key in the success of a new church. The church starter doesn't have to necessarily meet certain qualifications, as he or she has to have vision, drive, and commitment for the new church. Too often external qualifications actually impede the church-starting venture by disqualifying certain individuals who would be excellent church starters. Many of the church starters in the new churches featured in this chapter were not Southern Baptist or seminary trained before starting a Southern Baptist church. They did not meet "textbook requirements." But often these were the best church starters because they had the heart for the task. They learned and fulfilled the other external qualifications as they fulfilled their vision of building a church.

7. The sponsoring church can sponsor more than one church at a time. Although Brentwood did not sponsor all eight churches simultaneously, it did sponsor several churches at one time. Sponsorship of several churches at a time is possible because sponsorship should mean something different in each situation. Sponsorship often, but not always, means financial commitment. Where sponsorship does not involve large financial commitments, such as Brentwood Baptist Church's sponsorship of Heart of Houston Baptist Church, the sponsoring church is able to sponsor more than one church simultaneously.

8. *A new church must be accountable to its sponsoring church*. Likewise, the sponsoring church has a certain accountability to the new church. Accountability must be built into the covenant between the new church and the sponsoring church. The new church and sponsoring church are in a partnership to reach people for Christ. Brentwood Baptist Church is holding Heart of Houston Baptist Church pastor Doug Tipps accountable to his dream of a racially and economically balanced team of church leaders. Brentwood is also doing its part to help make that dream a reality.

9. *The development of lay leadership should be a top priority for any new church*. As churches grow, the pastors quickly learn that they cannot do everything. Pastors must believe in word and deed that each layperson is a minister. A church limits itself if it does not equip its laypeople. Faith Baptist Church members enter their community to witness and minister. Much of what the members do could not be accomplished by the pastor. They reach out to their neighbors and friends, and the church grows.

10. *The longer the tenure of the pastor, the greater the likelihood of success for the church*. In the new churches represented in this chapter, when a pastor left numbers dwindled, at least temporarily. Although many churches ultimately regained the numbers lost, some of the individuals following the pastor were never regained. Pastors must be encouraged to persevere, to stick with it, to live out their

commitment. Sponsoring churches can point new church pastors to the broader vision of the kingdom of God when circumstances seem insurmountable.

The ten churches presented in this chapter have gone before us. They have demonstrated that, despite whatever odds may present themselves, "It can be done!"

Notes

1. Beverly Trader, *Zion!* (unpublished play, 1990), 10.
2. Trader, op. cit., 11.
3. Trader, op. cit., 11.
4. Trader, op. cit., 11.
5. Trader, op. cit., 14.
6. Trader, op. cit., 23.
7. Trader, op. cit., 25.
8. Trader, op. cit., 34.
9. Trader, op. cit., 58.
10. Trader, op. cit., 29.
11. Trader, op. cit., 73.
12. Trader, op. cit., 72.
13. Margaret Dempsey, "Brentwood: Building Churches from Dreams," *Missions USA* (Atlanta: Home Mission Board, September-October 1991), 38-40.
14. Dempsey, op. cit., 36-38.
15. Dempsey, op. cit., 40.
16. Leisa A. Hammett, "Michael Cox: Profile of a Black Church Starter," *Churches Ministering to Black America* (Atlanta: Home Mission Board), 36-39.

3

Sharpening
Our Vision

We have seen examples of how others have journeyed down this road. Our journey must also begin with a vision of what could be, but what is not yet. This vision must be God-given, and it must reign supreme. Even when everything surrounding the vision, such as budget, facility, resources, seems to be working against it, the vision can continue to inspire and drive us in planting a church.

One critical mistake many church planters make today is to sacrifice their vision for the sake of a "model." We are "model hungry." Numerous model conferences are planned annually. Would-be church planters flock faithfully to these conferences, diligently taking notes, making a to-do list in their heads of how to go home and replicate that model in their communities.

Yet such a strategy doesn't work over the long haul. Models are important; they are created and designed to bring a vision to reality. Yet models are not supreme; the vision is supreme.

Many a church planter has given up in despair when the chosen model ceases to work, when it ceases to reach people. Yet if a vision were foundational for the church planter, that church planter would quite pragmatically realize that a model can change. In spite of the model change, the vision can remain constant.

A good example of a vision driving a new church start is Heart of Houston Baptist Church, a mission of Brentwood Baptist Church in Houston, Texas. Mission pastor Doug Tipps's vision is to start an inner-city church for people of all races and economic backgrounds—one that would proclaim the gospel when and where it was not expected. His model for fulfilling his vision has included renting a neutral location accessible to the people he wants to reach, developing a racially balanced church staff, and performing ministry in the inner city, such as adopting schools. Yet these models are expendable. When one proves fruitless, it can be replaced by a more appropriate model. For example, if Tipps were to discover that the location being used for the church was attracting only one segment of the audience he had hoped to attract, he could systematically discover why that particular location was not working and find another more suitable location.

The vision becomes the driving force behind which models are tried and used, which are never tried, and which are tried and discarded.

This chapter addresses how to develop and sharpen such a vision so that it is what moves and motivates us in our church-planning task. Several key elements contribute to the overall vision of starting a church. Many of these elements are basic and obvious. Yet, many are forgotten.

Burden for Lost People

The church planter must have a burden for lost people. "And seeing the multitudes, He felt compassion for them" (Matt. 9:36, NASB). Such must be the sincere attitude of the church planter.

Hundreds of church planters are at work across this country. Many diligently minister and witness relentlessly. Their burden for lost people compels them. They have no choice.

Yet many other church planters labor diligently, not out of a burden for lost people, but out of a burden for their own needs for success, for their own need to pastor large churches, for their own need for ambition. These church planters labor and they probably reach some people along the way. But, eventually, their burden will drive them away from church starting, perhaps even away from God.

The same misguided priorities exert control in sponsoring churches of new churches. Many sponsoring churches in our country are driven by a burden for lost people. They sincerely embrace a kingdom vision—realizing there are people to be reached for Christ who may never come to their established church but may attend a new church. These established churches sacrificially give of themselves, expecting nothing in return except the satisfaction of knowing they are doing something to reach lost people for Christ.

Many other sponsoring churches enthusiastically agree to help start new churches. Yet the burden is not for lost people. The burden is for recognition from their peers. These churches do all they can to let others know of their works and to ensure that they get much-deserved recognition. Yet soon the recognition dies down, and this church finds another pet project.

To develop a lasting vision for church planting, the church planter—and everybody else involved in starting a church, including the sponsoring church as well as new church members—must have a burden for lost people. The cries of the city, the cries of the homeless, the cries of

America must burden the church planter until something is done to reach these lost people for Christ.

Willingness to Develop and Participate in the Vision

The church planter must have, and be willing to participate in, a vision of what could be. The church planter must believe without hesitation that the lost people for whom he or she is burdened can be reached for Christ. As this vision begins to take shape, the church planter must yield to it. The church planter must move from having the vision to hearing the call to participate in that vision.

The church planter must also move from having the vision to developing the vision. The church planter must clarify or narrow the vision. In clarifying the vision, the church planter can ask, "What needs are present in this community? What need does this community have that nobody else is filling or is doing well at filling?" Then the church planter can find a niche. He or she can find a way to become a valuable resource in the community.

Sometimes the need that is not being met in a community translates into groups that are not being ministered to. For example, churches may be neglecting senior adults, single adults, middle-aged adults, or the middle-income crowd. If there is a group in the community that is being overlooked, that may very well be the cornerstone of the church vision.

One current phenomenon across the country is to build a church around the vision of reaching people who have turned their backs on traditional churches. There are enough people who fall out of traditional churches, who have fallen through the cracks of traditional churches, to fill up new churches all across the country. If the church planter can find common threads for these people, they can be brought into the church.

Ability to Sell the Vision

The church planter must sell the vision. The church planter must be sold and convinced that, whatever the vision, it can be done, must be done, and will be done through Christ. The church planter must be convinced that the new church can make a difference in the community. The church planter must be able to look someone in the eyes and say, "I need you. You need this vision." And that person walks away saying, "I need to do this."

Selling a vision is generally couched in the personality of the church planter. However, this does not necessarily mean the church planter has to have a vibrant, slap-on-the-back, gregarious personality. Rather, the church planter must have a communicating personality, a listening personality, a people personality. The church planter must be serious and sincere about the vision.

As the vision for a new church is transferred to the people, the church planter must be prepared. This preparation involves three crucial areas.

First, the church planter, much like a salesperson, must have full knowledge of the "product." The product, in this case, would be the new church. The target audience for the new church, much like a consumer, cannot know more than the salesperson about the product and what the product can or cannot do. Much of this knowledge grows out of the time the church planter has invested in studying the area and its needs.

Second, the church planter must have full knowledge of the target audience. The church planter must know so much about the people to be reached that he or she can go into the community with a sense of confidence. The church planter must know the people—their strengths, weaknesses, interests. The church planter presents the vision in a way that the target audience will at least be open to hearing it.

Third, the church planter must have full knowledge of obstacles, barriers, and resistance to the vision. Every visionary meets resistance. A visionary is able to look through the clouds and see the sun, to look through the storm and see the sun. The visionary must know that obstacles will exist. At the same time, the visionary must be able to present the product to the target audience in spite of these obstacles.

The visionary should anticipate the obstacles and be prepared with answers. In that way, the visionary can build the answers to these obstacles into the presentation of the vision. Often, questions can be answered before they are asked.

As the vision for a new church is transferred to the people, the church planter must be familiar with group dynamics. Group dynamics would dictate the following principles.

First, the church planter should "test" the vision with one or two trusted people. As the church planter shares the vision with these people, they will bring an evaluation, analysis, or appraisal of the vision. These responses will help the church planter tighten up or bring more clarity to the vision. Out of this process, the church planter gains one or two allies. The church planter can then go, with a more defined vision, to other people who will offer responses to the vision and become allies.

The most effective way to gain allies is to go to people personally. This gives people a personal stake in the vision and an opportunity to contribute something positive to it.

Also through this process, the church planter brings people together who may not normally cooperate with each other. For example, person A may not ordinarily work in a positive way with person B. However, because each has been enlisted individually, they no longer see each other as adversaries but as team players. Perhaps person A thinks person B has finally been convinced to see the right thing. Whatever the reason, personal enlistment is a successful way to bring people, who would normally have tensions with each other, together in a positive way.

Second, the church planter should present the vision to the corporate group. This presentation is made for affirmation, for commitment, and, most importantly, for ownership. The corporate group is the group that the church planter has nurtured and developed either from door-to-door campaigns, from one-on-one conversations, or from the church planter's allies bringing their friends to the opportunities for vision presentation.

This presentation to the corporate group is vital to the life of the vision. Often church planters have begun to build a core group for a church, for example with a home Bible study, but have not clarified their vision for a church. When this happens, some people, who may have been very active in a home Bible study, run the other way when they hear the word *church* for the first time. They say, "We wanted just a Bible study. We really weren't looking for a church."

The converse is also true. Some church planters have begun to build a core group, for example with a home Bible study, have shared the overall vision for starting a church, but have not given specifics. When this happens, some people in the Bible study become overly anxious to start the church immediately. A part of sharing the vision in a corporate group includes sharing pieces of the game plan along the way as well. The church planter thus gives the people a sense of the time line and process involved in starting the church.

Conclusion

The church planter must be committed to the God-given vision. Sometimes the obstacles will be overwhelming. Sometimes the church planter will feel rejected. But the church planter cannot stop seeing or articulating the vision. Continuing to see and articulate the vision, in spite of circumstances, takes perseverance and tenacity. Being true to the vision and to the God who calls the church planter to that vision is necessary to our journey in church planting.

4

Understanding the Role of the Sponsoring Church

The journey to begin a church in a predominantly black community should not be made in isolation, but rather in partnership. The most effective new works in any community are those that are done in the framework of a prayerful committed relationship between a sponsoring church and a new church.

Two definitions are helpful at this point. A sponsoring church—also known simply as a sponsor—is any congregation that has made a formal agreement to provide one or more resources for a specified period of time to help establish a viable, self-sufficient autonomous body of believers. Resources may include money, facility, teaching helps, leaders, or other things that would help the new church to survive and to grow. A new church—also known as a mission, a chapel, or a new work—is a young congregation that has not reached the level of maturity or financial self-sufficiency to exist apart from outside assistance.

Often, the sponsoring church/new church relationship is described in parental terms. The sponsoring church is the parent in the relationship. The new church is the child, usually known as the daughter congregation, in the relationship. While such a description offers interesting analogies, it is generally inappropriate for describing a cross-cultural sponsorship. Such sponsorships are inherently laden with issues of superiority and inferiority, independence and dependence. Any description or language that could bring these issues to the forefront, such as the parental model of sponsorship, should be avoided.

The relationship should be described in terms of a partnership. The sponsoring church and new church are partners together in reaching people who have not been reached for Christ. The new church could not do this task on its own. Neither could the sponsoring church do this task on its own. Each needs the other.

Excuses for Not Sponsoring Churches

While a church can realize great dividends in the kingdom of God through the sponsorship of a new work, many healthy, strong churches who are able to sponsor new works are unwilling to do so. Here are a few reasons why established churches are unwilling to become sponsoring churches:

"Somebody Else Will Do It"

This is a dangerous attitude that seems almost hereditary within church families. The corporate church that assumes another will take the responsibility in sponsoring a new work has little integrity when asking or expecting church members to take responsibility in the church. Individual church members have practiced making similar assumptions for years. "If I don't teach Sunday School, then somebody else will." "If I don't give to the church, then somebody else will." All church leaders know the error of individual church members in making these assumptions. It is a similar erroneous assumption for churches to assume somebody else will fulfill their responsibility in starting churches. More often than not, the responsibility goes unfulfilled, and God's plans are thwarted by a seemingly innocent assumption.

Unwillingness to Pay the Price in Finances, Time, and Church Members

Sponsoring a new church is costly. A sponsoring church must be willing to give of itself. What it gives will differ from situation to situation. However, a sponsoring church is often expected to give investments of money, time, and sometimes even church members as it helps establish a new church. Yet new churches are not given the "keys to the bank" of a sponsoring church. New churches are not allowed to indiscriminately drain a church's financial and human resources for its own benefit. As a sponsoring church and a new church enter into a relationship, the two should enter into a written agreement or covenant (discussed later in this chapter) outlining exact commitments of time, finances, and people between the two churches. Thus, a sponsoring church will not become overburdened or overextended as it seeks to establish a new church.

Lack of Understanding of a Kingdom Vision

Rather than an attitude that says, "We're all in this together," many churches develop a "We versus everybody else" attitude. While such an isolationist attitude has occasional political attraction, it has no place in the church. It cannot be upheld scripturally.

Christians are first and foremost citizens of the kingdom of God rather than members of an individual church. Churches should invest at least as much effort into growing the kingdom of God as they do in growing their churches.

How does growing the kingdom of God differ from growing a church? Essentially, growing the kingdom of God means that a church gives itself in ministering to and sharing the good news with individuals who may never join the local church or make any kind of contribution to it. Growing a church means the church once again gives itself in ministering to and sharing the good news with individuals, but this time, the individuals are subtly expected to give something back to the church, usually in terms of becoming a member.

Sometimes a church understands the concept of a kingdom vision but refuses to accept it. This church becomes self-idolatrous. A church is so consumed with itself and its own preservation that it cannot see beyond itself. Such a self-absorption backfires and hurts the church that is trying so desperately to protect itself. Randy Pope, pastor of Perimeter Presbyterian Church in Atlanta, Georgia, labels this a "meistic philosophy"[1] where church members become insistent upon their needs being met first before the church even considers going into the community to minister, evangelize, or start churches.

Fear of Diminishing Returns

Closely tied into the unwillingness to pay the price is the fear that the sponsoring church will pay a great price in starting a church but will realize little in return, perhaps even experience a loss on its investment. This is an attitude in which the church mirrors societal trends and responses rather than basing its trends and responses upon Scripture.

Yet a church seriously involved in church starting must admit the possibility of diminishing returns is real. Sometimes a sponsoring church expends much time, effort, and money into a new church that struggles along and never quite makes it on its own.

Although possible, diminishing returns are not probable. More often a sponsoring church is rewarded in seeing many people become Christians and involved in a local church.

No Vision for New Work

Many existing churches do not understand why new churches are needed. A prevalent belief is that there are enough existing churches to accommodate whoever wants to go to church. If an unchurched person were serious about wanting to go to church, then he or she could easily find an existing church to attend. Those with no vision for new work insist that rather than putting resources into starting churches, Christians should put resources into strengthening existing churches. Impassioned and impressive arguments are made on this point.

Yet, any twentieth-century American—churched or unchurched—knows that people want choices. If one word could describe contemporary American culture, it would be *choices*. A simple trip to the grocery store confirms this. The sheer numbers of shampoos, cereals, or dog food available can be overwhelming.

If people have such choice and variety in these inconsequential matters, then they come to expect, and they deserve choice and variety in churches.

One church simply cannot appeal to every person in a community. If a church seriously wants to reach its community for Christ, then it must realize that it cannot do it by itself. Some new churches must be started to reach specific cross sections of the community. To help start these new churches, existing churches must be willing to give of themselves.

Profile of a Healthy Sponsoring Church

In describing the kind of congregation that would make a healthy sponsoring church, the most obvious step would be to turn around the negative excuses for not starting churches. Thus, a healthy sponsoring church would display the following characteristics:

1. *Acceptance of its responsibility in starting a church.*—The sponsoring church must believe that if it does not sponsor a church, then a church probably will not be sponsored and people will not be reached with the good news.

2. *Willing to pay the price in finances, time, and church members.*—The sponsoring church must be willing to invest itself in the life of the new church.

3. *Commitment to a kingdom vision.*—The sponsoring church must understand and accept that it may not grow as a result of starting a church, but that the kingdom of God will grow.

4. *Acceptance of possibility of diminishing returns.*—Although diminishing returns are not the norm for sponsoring churches, the sponsoring church must be open to the risk. It must be ready to accept the possibility of not realizing immediate return on its investment.

5. *Vision for new work.*—The healthy sponsoring church must have a vision for reaching its community. To do that, the existing church must be open to building a variety of churches to reach the various people in its community.

Beyond these characteristics, the healthy sponsoring church exhibits several other traits that help make the relationship between sponsoring church and new church mutually satisfying:

Courage

Starting a church is a courageous step of faith. The sponsoring church must have courage to start a church in a community that may be totally different from the community in which it exists and among people who are different from its members. Most church members are secure in a cocoon of likeness. They work, live, play, and go to church with people who are like them. To start a church among people of a different race, culture, socioeconomic status, or whatever takes tremendous courage. It mandates leaving the cocoon and entering the world.

The sponsoring church also must have courage to start a church in a community that, from all outward appearances, may already have enough churches. The sponsoring church may meet critics who question the need for another church. Many of these critics will even be brothers and sisters in the faith who fear a loss of members in their churches or unwanted competition from a new church in the community. The sponsoring church must have courage to meet these critics, not only with love, but also with hard data, proving why a new church is needed.

The sponsoring church also must have courage to invest its resources in what could be considered a risky venture. Many unknowns are inherent in starting a church. A sponsoring church must be willing to say, "Whatever the outcome, this church is going to invest itself in the life of this new church."

Flexibility

A sponsoring church must be flexible in its approach to starting a new church. The most effective sponsoring church realizes that every situation is unique. What works in one situation may not work in another. What worked yesterday may not work today. The church that wishes to start another church is on the cutting edge of change and innovation. It must be ready to respond at a moment's notice when opportunities present themselves. It must be willing to change its methods of reaching people, if necessary, without changing its essential message. In doing so, it will follow the model of Jesus when He was on earth.

Selflessness

The sponsoring church must realize that in many ways it is giving itself away so that others might hear Christ's message. Starting a church means that the sponsoring church is putting its community first. It is thinking more of its community and the people who need to be reached than it is thinking of itself—its comfort, its bank account, its church rolls.

Openness

Closely tied to the trait of flexibility is the trait of openness. A sponsoring church must be open to new ideas and new ways of doing things. Because the new church does not have a history, it cannot say, "We never did it this way before." Because the sponsoring church wants to help the new church build a strong foundation for making its own history, it must not use those words either. The sponsoring church walks a fine line between using its years of experience and wisdom to offer helpful counsel to a new church and using its ingrained routines to force unnecessary conformity upon a new church. The sponsoring church should strive for the former and guard against the latter.

If the sponsoring church is a different cultural background from the new church, the sponsoring church must be open to the value and worth of different cultural expressions of the same gospel.

Special Challenges of a Cross-Cultural Sponsorship

In many instances the sponsor of a new church in a predominantly black community will be a church with a different cultural background. Building a sponsoring church/new church relationship between churches of different cultural backgrounds presents many special challenges.

One challenge in any cross-cultural sponsorship is to ensure that mutual understandings exist on terms used by the sponsoring church and new church. For example, the term "resources" may mean money to one church and literature to another church. In building a cross-cultural relationship, one key is to never assume anything. Give as much attention as possible to details, definitions, and other tools to help build understanding.

Another challenge in a cross-cultural sponsorship is to develop mutual understandings between the sponsoring church and new church on the potential of the new church. Often, individuals from different cultures would describe a "successful" church in different ways. For example, the sponsoring church may have a vision of the new church becoming a large, self-supporting church in a short period of time. However, if the new church is targeted to a small and perhaps low socioeconomic segment of the community, it may remain small and may require financial assistance for an extended period of time. Yet, though small and financially struggling, the new church could still be termed successful. In setting goals regarding the direction and future of the new church, both the sponsoring church and new church should be as precise and realistic as possible.

A third challenge in a cross-cultural sponsorship is for both sponsoring church and new church to acknowledge and respect differing styles of worship and spiritual expression. The history of African Americans in this country is directly tied to a unique worship style. A sponsoring church should not expect a new church to forego years of cultural history and identity to please the sponsoring church. Likewise, a new church should not be critical or derisive if a sponsoring church chooses to worship God differently.

A fourth challenge in a cross-cultural sponsorship is for both sponsoring church and new church to acknowledge and respect differing church priorities. For example, black churches historically have had a strong commitment to Christian social ministry—which is not an option for these churches, if they are to actually "be the church" in society. Sponsoring churches should accept this priority, realizing that this new church with its strong emphasis on ministry is still a Bible-believing, gospel-preaching church.

A fifth challenge in a cross-cultural sponsorship is for both sponsoring church and new church to allow each other the freedom to explore relationships with other churches. For example, a black church may choose to enter into a fellowship with other black churches, some of which may not be Southern Baptist. Rather than seeing this as a threat to its relationship with the new church, the sponsoring church should understand that such a fellowship speaks to needs that the sponsoring church may not be able to address. It offers a further environment in which the new church can grow and mature.

A sixth challenge in a cross-cultural sponsorship is the need to build trust. Unfortunately, little trust exists between cross-cultural groups in society today. At times, just when trust seems to be developing, something happens to upset the delicate balance. The challenge of building trust will require much time, prayer, perseverance, and honesty.

Trust will not be built overnight. Trust will not be built without Spirit-led words and actions. Trust will not be built without the commitment to "stick with it," despite the costs. Trust will not be built without some heart-wrenching, brutal honesty. And, most importantly, churches will not be built without trust.

A seventh challenge in a cross-cultural sponsorship is for the two churches and their leaders to develop and understand expectations for each other. For example, the sponsoring church may expect the new church to provide written monthly reports regarding church activities, attendance, financial matters, and so forth. Yet, this is largely an Anglo expectation. For some black church leaders, such an expectation seems unnecessary and a nuisance. The two churches should decide upon certain nonnegotiable expectations for their relationship and then strive to honor those expectations.

Guidelines for Sponsoring Church/New Church Relationships

For a healthy, mutually satisfying relationship to develop between the sponsoring church and new church, certain guidelines must be agreed upon by all parties involved. To prevent potential misunderstandings, these guidelines should be set forth in a covenant, a written document of agreement. The covenant should set forth expectations and responsibilities of both the sponsoring church and new church.

Everyone involved in the process should understand that the new church is a part of the sponsoring church. Although the new church may meet in a different place and reach a different group of people, it still operates under the governance and authority of the sponsoring church until it becomes a constituted, autonomous church on its own.

In developing the covenant, the sponsoring church and the new church should consider the following significant topics:

Church Membership

Members of the new church are actually members of the sponsoring church. Therefore, those who desire membership in the mission must meet the membership requirements of the sponsoring church. The mission may receive members on behalf of the sponsoring church. Those joining the mission should join by one of these methods: (1) by baptism, after profession of faith, (2) by letter from another Southern Baptist church, or (3) by statement of faith and statement of baptism. The clerk of the sponsoring church should maintain a membership list for the mission.

The sponsoring church may want to be available to provide new member orientation/training classes for those who join the mission.

Members of any of the program organizations of the new church are also actually members of the program organizations of the sponsoring church. This may include Sunday School, Discipleship Training, Woman's Missionary Union, Brotherhood, and Church Music. The sponsoring church may want to provide leadership in establishing and developing any program organizations that the new church desires.

Pastor

The new church and the sponsoring church should agree on the new church's pastor. A written document outlining principles, procedures, and guidelines for a joint pastor-search committee could provide structure for this process. Even if the mission currently has a pastor, the document should be prepared so it is available if needed in the future.

Just as with church members, the pastor of the new church is a member of the sponsoring church. Further, he is considered a staff member of the sponsoring church. The pastor of the new church and the pastor of the sponsoring church should develop a close relationship. The two should meet regularly to discuss goal-setting, expectations, plans, activities, and evaluation. The pastor of the sponsoring church should prayerfully work with the pastor of the new church to help him develop vision, mission, and direction.

Equipment and Property

Equipment and property are maintained in the name of the sponsoring church until the mission constitutes into a church. At that time, the equipment and property, along with any liabilities, are transferred to the new church.

The sponsoring church can provide a great service to the new church that is looking at its physical facility by emphasizing that the congregation is not a *place*. The sponsoring church can help the new church look at alternative meeting places and the financial obligations they create.

The new church will want to pace itself and not overextend itself. At the time the new church is constituted, it should be able to maintain its location financially.

Church Missions Development Council (Formerly Church Missions Committee)

The church Missions Development Council represents the sponsoring church and should meet monthly with the mission pastor and one or more elected representatives from the mission. These meetings provide opportunity for reports, planning, and prayer for the mission. The Missions Development Council reports to the sponsoring church regarding the mission's needs and plans.

Business Meetings

The mission should hold regular business meetings to discuss and vote on matters of business which will then be given to the sponsoring church for approval. These business meetings would include nomination and election of officers and leaders for the mission.

Church Ordinances

The observances of the church ordinances, baptism and the Lord's Supper, should be conducted in accordance with the sponsoring church's constitution or approval. The mission pastor and sponsoring church pastor should work together in planning observances of the ordinances.

Financial Matters

The mission should submit a recommended budget to the sponsoring church Missions Development Council, which, in turn, will recommend it to the sponsoring church for approval. Some stipulation should be agreed upon regarding nonbudget expenditures which would require sponsoring church approval. Monthly mission financial reports should be provided to the sponsoring church Missions Development Council.

The mission is urged to give a definite percentage of its tithes and offerings through the Cooperative Program. It should increase this percentage in the future. Additionally, the mission is urged to give a definite percentage of its tithes and offerings to associational missions.

The mission and sponsoring church should have a written understanding regarding the amount and duration of financial assistance the sponsoring church will be able to provide. Any stipulations regarding how the funds are to be used should also be agreed upon in writing. For example, the sponsoring church may provide funds specifically for facility rental; purchase of a building or property; construction of a building; pastor's salary, housing, or retirement; or purchase of curriculum, hymnals, or promotional materials.

When the mission is constituted into a church, all mission funds and liabilities become the property of the new church.

Reaching Maturity

When a congregation has become mature enough to govern itself and to be financially self-supporting, preparation should be made to constitute the mission into a self-governing church. There is no set timetable to when this should occur. Conceivably, some missions, because of their locations, constituency, or any number of reasons, may never be able to constitute into an autonomous church. The sponsoring church should be prepared to face this eventuality in rare cases.

Conclusion

To be a sponsoring church is a privilege and an honor. It offers a church a unique opportunity to become a partner with other believers to reach people for Christ. It often pumps new life and joy into an otherwise comfortable and sometimes lethargic congregation.

To be a sponsoring church is also an awesome responsibility and challenge. It demands selfless giving of valuable resources. Further, cross-cultural sponsorships demand breaking down stereotypes between cultural groups and hammering out relationships of respect and acceptance.

Regrettably, too many churches look no further than the staggering responsibility to determine if sponsoring a new congregation is for them. They give church starting only a fleeting thought—turning thoughts and energies inward. As in churches where the minority of church members do the vast majority of church work, these self-centered churches happily allow a committed minority of churches to do the majority of church starting. In so doing, they miss out on one of the most invigorating and rewarding ventures possible, bringing countless individuals into a saving relationship with Christ and into a local body of believers.

Note

1. From an address given by Randy Pope, pastor of Perimeter Presbyterian Church, Atlanta, Georgia, at Celebration '92, February 1992, in San Antonio, Texas.

5

Understanding the Role of the Church Planter

As Jesus journeyed toward the land of the Samaritans, so we must continue our journey to lands unknown. We cannot go as a loosely aligned group of people with varying abilities, interests, motivations, and commitments. Then our journey would become no more than random wanderings. To continue our purposeful journey, a leader must emerge. This leader will be able to mold our motley band of believers into a unified, visionary group. This leader is the pastor.

At first glance, it may seem obvious that a pastor is necessary to a church-starting venture. However, some may argue that if we believe in the priesthood of the believer, then we should not emphasize the pastor and his role in church starting. If all believers are on an equal plane in the sight of God and if all are rightfully seen as ministers, then cannot a group of committed, visionary laypeople start a church as well as a pastor can? The answer is yes, and no.

Stories abound on groups of lay believers who become burdened about communities and begin meeting in homes for prayer and Bible study. Soon these spontaneous prayer meetings give birth to churches and, somewhere along the way, pastors are called.

And these pastors are necessary to the continued growth and vitality of the new church. Although any believer who is connected with a new church is vital and has a specific role to fulfill as a minister of the gospel, the pastor is indispensable. Without a pastor convinced that a new church is needed and committed to giving whatever it takes to start that church, a new church would falter and probably fail. The pastor provides vision and leadership for his congregation and offers a worthy model of perseverance when circumstances may be discouraging.

Not just any pastor will do, however. Church starting in the black community takes the right pastor. The choice of pastor "usually is the most important decision in launching a new congregation," says church-growth specialist Lyle Schaller. He explains, "Frequently, the identity of that new church is a reflection of the personality, gifts, gender, values, experience, nationality, race, education, priorities, family status, political views, theological stance, social class, age, and hobbies of the pastor."[1]

The prominence of the pastor in the black church tradition is even more pronounced than in the white church tradition. "The central figure in the Black Church is the black preacher," C. Eric Lincoln says unequivocally.[2] "The black preacher includes a dimension peculiar to the black experience," he believes.[3]

That peculiar dimension can be likened to the historic role of the black tribal chieftain, a leader not only religiously, but also socially, culturally, and politically. The black preacher historically "was more than leader and pastor, he was the projection of the people themselves."[4] That historic tradition lives today, even for younger blacks who have little or no church experience. The black pastor is a spiritual leader, but he is also more.

Who is the right pastor for a new church in a predominantly black community? To answer that question, let us first examine who is *not* the right pastor.

First, the right pastor to start a church in a black community is *not* one who accepts the responsibility by default. We will refer to this person as Daniel Default. First, Daniel says one of two things, "I don't see a church out there that I want," or "No church has called me." In lieu of those two circumstances, Daniel then says, "So, at least for now, I'll try this. I'll start a church. If it doesn't work out, surely something else will come around eventually." In the absence of other pastoral opportunities, Daniel reluctantly accepts a church-starting assignment. Daniel has an attitude problem and that poor attitude would be translated into a less than satisfactory church-starting experience.

Second, the right pastor to start a church in the black community is *not* just anybody who is black. We will refer to this person as Byron Black. The color of Byron's skin becomes the sole criterion for determining if he is the right pastor for the new church. No consideration is given to other significant factors such as Byron's ability to relate to people, his identity with the community, or his theology.

One example of when a person's race obviously did not determine whether a person "fit in" a community was in the late 1950s when a large number of blacks were migrating from the South to the North. Those who went North did not merge into the existing black churches. Instead they started their own. The reason was simple. Blacks from the South were socially and culturally different from Northern blacks. If you were a black from Jackson, Mississippi, as opposed to Chicago, Illinois, that was an entirely different ball game. Other factors, equally as important as race, determined whether a person was comfortable in a community. Even today, some churches in the North have "state" clubs, such as the Mississippi Club, for church members from that particular state.

A person's race is important, but certainly not the only factor in selecting the right pastor for a new church. With such lack of consideration regarding the whole person selected as pastor, both the new church and the pastor would be entering into a precarious relationship at best.

Third, the right pastor to start a church in a black community is *not* the person with the most educational degrees beside his name. We will refer to this person as Edward Education. An obvious tendency for a sponsoring church is to consider only those candidates who have specific educational qualifications. After the rudimentary educational requirements imposed on candidates by the sponsoring church, those candidates with additional educational qualifications are viewed as superior.

As with the consideration of a person's race, education is an important factor in selecting a pastor, but certainly not the only one. Sometimes quality individuals are summarily dismissed as potential candidates simply because they do not meet the educational requirements. Rather than a rigid set of standards, a sponsoring church would do well to exercise sensitivity and openness to the Holy Spirit in matching the person with the context.

Two current trends support such fluidity. One trend is for older men to leave their careers and respond to calls to the ministry. Such men can easily attain the necessary educational qualifications even while they are in the ministry. A second trend is for missions to begin looking for a pastor or spiritual leader from within the congregation rather than elsewhere. Such a pastor would have already have the necessary vision and commitment that someone from outside the community of believers may not have.

If Daniel Default, Byron Black, and Edward Education are not the right persons for the new church, then who is? A sponsoring church should consider several factors. None of these are race specific, they are universal principles critical to the process of starting a church in a predominantly black community. They must be applied to each specific situation. Among these factors are the following.

The candidate and the community in which the new church is located must be compatible.—The two must be matched economically and socially as much as possible. The homogeneity/heterogeneity principle can be argued convincingly on both sides of the issue. However, the clear reality is that people tend to gravitate toward those like themselves. The more the new pastor becomes ingrained into the community and the community accepts him, the more likely the church is to reach people for Christ. For example, some men would work well in the inner city but would feel ill at ease in the suburbs, while others would be at home in the suburbs and would be totally out of place in the inner city. If someone is out of context socially and economically as he enters a new church community, it stands to reason that the relationship between the church and pastor would be potentially troublesome.

The key here is that the target community must be studied thoroughly before selecting a pastor for the new church. The complexity of the black community must be taken into account in selecting a pastor. Making broad generalizations or assumptions about a community just because its primary racial makeup is black is a serious error that could result in difficulties for the new church and pastor.

The new pastor must be able to exhibit adaptability, compatibility, and flexibility in relating to his neighborhood. Likewise, community residents, particularly new church members, must show an openness toward the new pastor and respect him as an individual.

The candidate and the sponsoring church must have a mutual understanding and commitment to their covenant relationship. —The sponsoring church must make an effort to explain the covenant relationship with the candidate. All involved need to understand what to expect from each other. This kind of understanding should be ironed out before the first dollar, the first acre of land, or the first anything is committed.

If such understandings are not worked out, the church planter may have a distorted understanding of accountability. Thus, when the sponsoring church requires a report or some other indicator of accountability, the church planter may cry "Foul," and accuse the sponsoring church of paternalism. Unfortunately, *paternalism* has become a catch word often applied to accountability.

The new church pastor should understand that members of the new church are technically members of the sponsoring church. That concept extends to the pastor, who is actually a staff member of the sponsoring church. When he sees his relationship in that perspective, the new church pastor is more likely to understand that he is accountable to the sponsoring church. The sponsoring church has a right and an obligation to know what is going on in the new church.

New churches in black communities, sponsored by predominantly white churches, seem to have a bigger problem with this issue than churches in black communities sponsored by other black churches. Black church leaders and members have come to expect an attitude of paternalism from their white counterparts, so when anything even resembling accountability occurs, the charges are paternalism. This is especially true among black Christians who come from a non-Southern Baptist background. However, the problem also occurs in black churches sponsored by black churches. The most effective deterrent to this problem is for both the new church pastor and the sponsoring church to have a clear understanding regarding the terms of the relationship before anything is formalized.

The new church pastor must have a holistic vision of planting churches.—As sponsoring churches interview potential candidates for the new church pastorate, questions need to be raised about each candidate's vision of ministry of church planting. Ideally, the new church pastor should have the attitude, "Not only do I want to plant a church, but I also want to plant a church that will plant a church." He should be able to articulate the belief, "Not only do I believe in starting churches so that I can become the pastor of a great church, but I also believe that there are lost people outside the context which I will reach, who need and deserve to be reached as well."

Why is it important that the new church pastor articulate that type of vision? Several reasons can be cited. First, the pastor has been the recipient of such a vision on the part of the sponsoring church, and he should be able to give to others as he has received from others. Second, enlisting new church pastors with a "kingdom vision" helps to build an army of people committed to starting churches where there are lost people. Nothing less than such an army will come close to tackling Southern Baptists' church-planting task. Third, the pastor with a kingdom vision for starting churches will be able to withstand the storms and difficulties that most certainly will come in his church-starting venture. Those with a broader vision are better equipped to handle minor setbacks and crises than are those who can only see the "here and now."

The new church pastor must be willing to diligently study his community in order to ascertain the kind of church the community needs.—The new church pastor must know the pulse beat of the community where the church is to be planted, from which a specific church-starting strategy will be developed. Too often, our church-planting strategy has been the exact opposite. Our strategy has exhibited nothing new and has not been community specific. The attitude has been, "I'm just going to put up a building and open up for business on Sundays." That kind of strategy will go nowhere in the black community.

The new church pastor must first look at the general demographics available on the area and its residents. Such information might include data on income level, family makeup, educational background, type of housing, age, male-female ratios, number of children. The associational director of missions has ready access to much of this information. The role of the sponsoring church is to help the new church pastor interpret this data accurately. This kind of information is necessary and helpful; it answers many questions, but it is not enough.

The new church pastor must also ascertain information about the community that cannot be read on a page. He must be willing to walk with the community residents, to listen, to learn. He must be able to articulate and believe and probably be consumed by the needs of the community. He must be able to answer the question of why another church is needed in that particular community.

The most successful new churches will target the most critical needs in the community. One example of targeting critical needs is a mission of Brentwood Baptist Church, Houston, Texas. A critical need in the community was to minister to children with sickle-cell anemia who, because of their illness, were forced to miss school frequently. The mission has begun a ministry using volunteers to tutor these children in their homes when they were absent from school.

Jesus is our model in sensitively speaking to needs. He knew the people to whom He was ministering; to whom He was presenting the gospel. And He tailored His message to fit their needs. The new church pastor must do the same.

The new church pastor should also understand that as he begins the church, his vision or strategy for the church may not be complete. And it probably will not be complete for some time. The people who respond to the church in its early years will do a lot to create and develop the personality of the church.

The contemporary terminology for this is market segmentation. It is a valid concept for church planting.

The new church pastor must be a risk taker.—Starting a church, especially a church to meet community needs, is risky business. One runs the risk of being misunderstood, of being seen as competition from existing churches, of being ignored. It is not as big a risk for the new church pastor to start a church that is a duplication of what every other church looks like. But it is a large risk to start a church that offers something new, that is a new model of "church." And that's exactly the kind of church that is destined to be most successful in terms of reaching people. The new church pastor must be willing to lead his church in daring to minister in this area when it is safer to stay inside the four walls of the church.

How willing is the new church pastor to be a risk taker? Does the new church pastor see risks as problems or as opportunities? How creative is the pastor in developing a church relevant for today's society?

The new church pastor must like people.—This characteristic for the new church pastor seems trite. It seems so obvious that it does not need to be stated. Unfortunately, that is not always the case. Good, sincere men have entered the ministry, but it soon became obvious that they simply did not care deeply about other people. Their ministries were doomed to failure. The sponsoring church should try to ensure that the new church pastor exudes Christ's love and concern for others.

The new church pastor must make a tremendous commitment to the church-starting task.—Church starting is not a casual undertaking. It is not for the fainthearted or easily discouraged. The new church pastor must have a burning passion for new work. He must make a similar commitment to his task as a foreign missionary would make—to go in and do what he was called to do in spite of the odds. A new church pastor must yield to the call God has given him, to the commitment God requires of him, to the passion Jesus demands of those who are going to love His people.

As our journey, church starting in black communities, continues, the new church pastor must affirm that the black community does not need any more mediocre churches. It needs churches that will make a difference. The new pastor must dedicate himself to making that affirmation a reality.

Notes

1. Lyle E. Schaller, *Forty-Four Questions for Church Planters* (Nashville: Abingdon Press, 1991), 108.

2. C. Eric Lincoln, ed., *The Black Experience in Religion* (Garden City, N.Y.: Anchor Books, 1974), 65.

3. Ibid.

4. Lincoln, op. cit., 67.

6

Surviving the Obstacle Course

The twists and turns, ups and downs of our journey become increasingly evident the further we travel. These are the obstacles of starting and growing churches in predominantly black communities. Although expected, they are not welcomed. Although disheartening, they do not have to be life-threatening. Although seemingly ever-present, they must not become our intimate traveling companions.

There are several common obstacles that those involved in starting and growing churches in predominantly black communities may encounter. These are presented with the hope that churches and church leaders will be better prepared to tackle each issue as it presents itself.

The Numbers Game

"The bottom line." "Risk management." These are the buzz words of the latter part of the twentieth century. But can such concepts apply to our church-starting task? In a sense, they cannot apply. In another sense, they must.

Numbers come into play in at least two areas in church starting.

Where Is a New Church Needed?

How does one determine where a new church is needed? Demographics and statistics must be considered. Church-to-population ratios present telling evidence about the needs for churches. These numbers present solid, objective information—the type of information that denominational decision makers must consider in order to make difficult decisions about where to place resources. Where the need is objectively obvious, a response is given.

Yet, objective information is not the only consideration in determining where to start a church. A certain subjectivity must be allowed. Often God leads an individual to sense needs and to feel burdened to meet those needs. This subjectivity cannot be quantified or packaged; neither can it be denied.

Generally, denominational decision makers have been more inclined toward considering quantifiable data in determining where a new church is needed. Because these people are not on the mission field where needs are obvious, this is a reliable method of research. Those in the hands-on ministry have been more inclined toward the subjective realization of a need. They do not have the luxury of cross tabulations showing where churches and people are located.

To determine the need for churches in black communities, neither approach should be used exclusively. Using one to the exclusion of the other is a trap that could mean that some churches which are desperately needed are not started. Both approaches are necessary if used correctly.

Numbers can help us to become more attuned to the leadership of God's Holy Spirit, but they have also been used to effectively squelch that leadership. Those with the authority to make decisions about where to plant churches must not allow statistics to undermine God's leadership of individuals.

Conversely, those who realize a need through prayer and communion with God can proclaim God's desires more clearly than anyone, but these individuals at times have doggedly denied that God could lead through statistics or actually speak to denominational decision makers. Potential church planters should not negate the tremendous tool of statistical and demographic information that God provides.

Determining where a new church is needed is a both/ and proposition. God leads objectively through statistics and demographics. God also leads subjectively through individuals sensing a burden.

A good example of how God can lead both subjectively and objectively is Brentwood Baptist Church in Houston, Texas, where author Joe Ratliff serves as pastor. In 1965 when an existing church was considering the start and sponsorship of Brentwood, statistics supported the new-church start, but in a limited way. The numbers revealed that people were moving to this bedroom community. Statistics further indicated the new church would be a community church, with a maximum membership of eight hundred people. In addition, deed restrictions placed the new church in an area of low visibility and relative inaccessibility—two factors that could mean trouble for any new church.

However, nothing in the statistics foreshadowed the impact that Brentwood would have on its entire city. Because of the subjective leadership and vision of its leaders and the undeniable involvement of the Holy Spirit, Brentwood is now a regional church with a membership of approximately eight thousand. The average church member drives fifteen miles to church. Brentwood itself has started seven churches in the past five and one-half years.

Once again, numbers must not be used to undermine the work of the Holy Spirit. We must listen to numbers and pay attention to statistics and other good information, but realize that God can transcend numbers.

Is the New Church Successful?

How does one determine the success of a new church? Once again, numbers must be considered but are not the sole, or perhaps even the best, consideration in determining the success of the new church. Using numbers to measure the success of a venture is, by and large, the secular approach that Christians have bought into. "Bigger is better." The emergence of the mega church in the 1980s and 1990s gives credence to this belief. But, for every mega church, there are two hundred smaller churches.

Which church is more successful? One which averages thousands of worshipers each Sunday morning and has the budget to air worship services on television? Or an inner-city church that struggles to have thirty-five attend on a Sunday morning and still receives a stipend from its sponsoring church after seven years? The answer is "none of the above." Neither church is more or less successful than the other. Each church is successful if it is being faithful to God in following the Great Commission.

Unfortunately, those of us involved in church starting, in an attempt to challenge a church to grow and to become self-supporting, often impose debilitating standards on it. If a church does not have the numbers or the financial resources to have a full-time pastor, staff, and all of those other things that "we want for our churches," then that church may be mistakenly labeled a failure. And, in all probability, the church will then attain that label.

What exactly do we want for our churches? As we answer that question, we find that what we want for our churches is greatly influenced by our mentors, past experiences, past pastorates, self-confidence, trust, and faith in people around us, and other factors. Thus, what we want is largely a product of our environment. Most church leaders agree on the substance of a new church start. When we start talking about form, however, is when we differ and tend to start assigning labels on ourselves and on others.

We must realize that not all churches will reach large numbers of people, have full-time pastors or staff, or even become self-supporting. But that is acceptable, because not all churches are alike.

We must also affirm that churches should be challenged to grow and to become all that God intends. Churches should be encouraged to set growth goals. Churches should be undergirded with support and affirmation so that they are able to do ministry and grow spiritually and perhaps numerically.

A church's success is measured through tangibles—number of church members, size of budget, and the like. A church's success is also measured through intangibles—an individual with a changed life, a ministry to the forgotten.

Looking Out for Number One

Looking out for number one—becoming egocentric—is a common obstacle faced not only by new churches in black communities but also by the denomination starting them. Once again, twentieth-century society—the "me" generation—presses in on churches and the denomination, compelling them to model society rather than to pattern their lives after Christ's.

New churches struggle to establish their identities, to raise budgets, perhaps to build facilities. New churches also face the skepticism and outright negativism of other churches, perhaps from other denominations, that may be in their communities. All of these reasons tempt churches to turn inward, keeping their resources and plans to themselves, while at the same time trying to reach outward into the communities.

While churches are wrestling with these challenges, the Southern Baptist Convention is doing the same. Ours is a denomination that has a history of questionable involvement in the black community. At times, our efforts as Southern Baptists to start churches in black communities seem to be sabotaged by our own history. Now our denomination is waging a major offensive to start churches in these communities. Skepticism and negativism on the local level are compounded immeasurably on the national level. As other denominations question the motives of the Southern Baptist Convention and remind us of our segregated history, the tendency is to turn inward, to take a "We-don't-need-them" attitude.

What is the answer to these challenges for churches and the denomination? First, acknowledge that what the Southern Baptist Convention is proposing is very aggressive. With this aggression comes what some would call arrogance. But, perhaps in sheer self-defense of the negative connotation of the word *arrogance,* let us use the term "confidence." This confidence must be kept in perspective. It must be a confidence in Christ, for what He has called us to do and for the power He provides, rather than self-confidence. Also, while acknowledging our history in the black community, we must confidently rise above it. We must patiently remind our critics, "That was then; this is now."

The second part of the answer is to develop a "kingdom vision." Churches must resist the tendency to turn inward. Churches must strive to be a part of their denomination—all the way from the association to the state to the national level. This may mean sacrifice in terms of time and money. It may also mean some skepticism from your own "folk," which is more difficult than suspicions from strangers. In the end, the benefits of being part of a larger family will outweigh the costs.

Churches must also strive to become part of the larger religious community—the very community that is not so sure you should be starting churches. While acknowledging that we feel called to serve God in this way at this time, we must also acknowledge that other churches and denominations have stakes in black communities as well. Southern Baptist churches that want to start congregations in black communities must be willing to be partners in winning a community to Christ, and to take an honest, nonpaternalistic approach to those who are already in the black community doing a good job. Southern Baptists must be willing to say, "What can we do together to reach this community for Christ? What can we learn from each other?" As church leaders become acquainted, share each other's burdens, and pray together, something will happen. A cohesiveness can develop. Suspicions may dissolve. People will be reached—and it won't really matter who reaches them.

The denomination must develop a kingdom vision. The Southern Baptist Convention must demonstrate genuine respect for other denominations, keep in mind that relationships will not develop immediately, and be willing to work at those relationships over the long haul.

While it is natural and necessary to look out for ourselves, we must not do so at the exclusion of others.

Plotting Our Own Futures

A major point of tension between a new congregation and an sponsoring church is that of allowing the new congregation to be itself, rather than to be a clone of the sponsoring church. This tension has caused many relationships to break down and others to never begin. What is the answer?

First, it is the role of the sponsoring church to educate the new congregation on what it means to be Southern Baptist. In so doing, the sponsoring church must be honest. It must not allow peripheral matters to invade or influence their interpretation of being Southern Baptist.

Second, the sponsoring church must allow the new congregation, in a sense, to chart its own destiny. The two congregations will share many commonalities; likewise, they will have many differences. An example of this is a church that author Michael Cox helped to plant. In this new congregation's budget were the traditional Southern Baptist items, such as Cooperative Program and associational missions. But one item in the budget differed greatly from anything the sponsoring church had ever had in its budget. The new congregation included in its budget a contribution to the United Negro College Fund. When the sponsoring church reviewed the budget, this contribution was immediately questioned. After an open conversation about how the new congregation felt a keen commitment to education in the black community and how this contribution helped to meet that commitment, the sponsoring church responded affirmatively. That's the way it should be.

Another example of a possible area of tension and/or misunderstanding between a sponsoring church and a new church is worship style. If the sponsoring church is an Anglo church with a traditional Southern Baptist worship service, expectations may revolve around the desire for the new church to conduct its worship service in a similar style. These expectations may come from either the perspective of the sponsoring church or the new church.

Rather than insisting that the worship style of the new church emulate that of the sponsoring church, however, both churches should allow worship to emanate. True worship emanates, rather than emulates. Traditional black worship has certain characteristics. It is highly participatory, features quality music, is spontaneous, and emphasizes preaching. However, all of these characteristics can be couched in various ways so that the worship style of the new church is truly its own.

A tendency for many sponsoring churches is to look upon the new congregation as a "baby." As the sponsoring church nurtures that new church, the desire becomes for that new church to resemble its sponsoring church in every way. Rather, the new church should be allowed to grow naturally and to become what God means for it to become. During this growth process, the sponsoring church could provide much-needed guidance and support.

There may be much give and take between a new congregation and its sponsoring church; there may be disagreements; there may be lengthy discussions and explanations. In the end, however, the sponsoring church should accept the new congregation's personality and grant it some measure of freedom to develop that personality.

The denominational structure must also allow churches in black communities to be themselves. Churches in black communities cannot be expected to emulate the qualities and actions of white churches. The "cookie-cutter mentality" that says, "You must look like me, act like me, walk like me," will not work as the Southern Baptist Convention steps into black communities.

Rehearsing or Reversing

Another common obstacle faced by a new church in the black community is how deeply to become involved in social issues. Most ministers in these churches are not reluctant to preach from the pulpit about the inhumanity or injustice of certain situations or issues. Church members encourage and expect such forthright preaching. But, without accompanying actions, the words become empty—a simple rehearsal rather than a reversal.

Throughout history the black church has vigorously seized the role of social activist. It has identified and has worked to meet community needs, issues, and problems. The black church has presented Jesus Christ not only as our eternal Savior but also as our contemporary Redeemer. The "cause" of Christ inspired the church to be outspoken and involved. At these times, the black church has been at its best. It has the attention and respect of the whole community because it initiated or activated positive social change.

As churches are started in black communities across our country today, each must examine its reason for being and its role in the community. New churches in black communities should be designed from their births with the intentions of not just rehearsing the realities from their pulpits and halls but of reversing those realities by getting involved in their communities and ministering. Churches designed with that purpose or scope develop a compelling presence in their communities and exhibit a magnetism for community residents.

Thinking About Tomorrow

"There seems to be a growing amount of evidence that next year is going to be 1991. If that's true, we've got problems. If it were going to be 1951, we might know what to do," said church-growth specialist Lyle Schaller, speaking to a group of metropolitan ministers in May 1990.[1]

Schaller lamented that most churches are stuck in a time warp that causes them to be thirty years behind current trends. Most church planters smugly nod their collective heads in agreement. *It's a shame that established churches are not more open to new outlooks,* they think.

But being in a time warp is not limited to established churches; new churches suffer from the same problem.

Starting new churches is not simply putting "new wine into old bottles" (Matt. 9:17). People do that because it's familiar and comfortable. The fear of failure will drive people to put together in a new church what was successful in the past. The problem is they do not take into consideration the historical context. They simply try to duplicate their past successes in a new era with new people. That is a mistake.

Church starters who try to institute traditional church life are often the ones whose churches struggle and stay mediocre. These are the church planters who try to implement status-quo patterns and reconstruct previous experiences in new contexts. They are, in effect, inflexible and insensitive to the people they are trying to reach.

On the other hand, church planters who dare to do something different are often the ones whose churches are really making a difference. These church planters adapt tradition and adopt patterns to accommodate the unchurched. They are flexible in allowing the new church's programs, worship times, ministries, and activities to reflect the needs of those they are trying to reach. In effect, these church planters are saying to the unchurched, "We want you. We want you badly enough to do whatever it takes, with the exception of changing our message, to reach you."

To avoid the temptation to "do church as it has always been done," a new church must seize the opportunity to create and mold its own life. The new church must resist being a replication of what has been. It must be willing to struggle and discover its purpose and possibilities. The church in the black community is generally open to the idea of innovation, of not being wed to tradition. But to make this concept work, the new church needs support from its sponsoring church.

The sponsoring church must embrace this concept of not doing business as usual. It must challenge the new church to do things differently, to be sensitive to the community and God's Word, to discover why God wants the new church in that particular community.

Going It Alone

Fear, uncertainty, pride, and distrust combine to influence a new congregation to "go it alone," to reject sponsoring-church assistance. A sponsoring church may not question the rejection, because it is experiencing some of the same negative feelings. Thus, sponsorship becomes "sponsorship on paper" only. The full richness of the relationship is never tapped. Much is lost. Much pain and struggle that could have been avoided are borne.

One reason for the significant negative feelings is that, traditionally, black churches have not started other churches with the direct support that Southern Baptists are offering. Black churches have been started with only the meager, limited resources of those who choose to affiliate with the new congregation. While churches in black communities could certainly find uses for Southern Baptists' wealth of resources, they are not sure why Southern Baptists are supposedly being so openhanded with this long-ignored group. Churches in black communities also want to resist the temptation to become affiliated with the Southern Baptist Convention because of the lure of abundant resources.

A reason why potential sponsoring churches harbor such negative feelings has to do with the challenge of cross-cultural sponsorship. White churches have little, if any, experience in black communities. They don't understand the black worship experience. When faced with even moderate resistance from black church starters, white church members too easily declare, "Fine, if 'they' want to do it on 'their' own, we'll let them."

The solution to this obstacle is not simple. It will take models of how a sponsoring church and a new congregation can link hearts and hands to reach a community for Christ. It needs people who are willing to try this approach and let others know about their successes and failures. One inroad into this arena could be linking new congregations with prayer sponsors. The two congregations could hold prayer meetings about new work, praying specifically for the new church members. Prayer could be a link. Although the two groups of people may pray differently, prayer is not only communication with God, it is therapeutic. Using prayer as focal point—seeking God's guidance and blessings—could do much to steer clear of this obstacle and to develop the new work.

Conclusion

No promises have been made that starting churches in black communities is easy or stress free. It takes effort, hard work, prayer, flexibility, preparation, openness, commitment, the list goes on. It may not be easy, but God's leadership is evident in this undertaking, and He will provide all that is needed.

In starting churches in black communities, be prepared to face the obstacles outlined in this chapter and perhaps others. As you face these obstacles, work through them. Do not let them detour you from your ultimate task. Look upon these obstacles as opportunities to grow and be stretched by God and others.

Note

1. From an address given by Lyle Schaller, church growth authority, at a Models for Metropolitan Ministry Conference, in Washington, D.C., in May 1990.

Appendix

First Baptist Greens Bayou

1. **Church Target Audience**
   Middle class
2. **Location**
   Suburb: lower middle class, older homes, and large concentration of apartments.
3. **Planter Profile**
   The Rev. M.E. Williams: BA, New Jerusalem Baptist Church, pastor, 1967-71; St. Peter's Baptist Church, pastor, 1971-73; Mount Rose Baptist Church, pastor, 1973-82; First Baptist of Greens Bayou, pastor, 1984-88
4. **Meeting Place History**
   Church facility in changing community
5. **Number of People Initially Involved**
   9
6. **Membership History**
   1st year—190
   2nd year—450
   3rd year—850
   4th year—1,110
   5th year—500
   6th year—800

7th year—1,100
8th year—1,500
7. **Person(s) Responsible for Initiating Plant**
   Planter initiated
8. **Start-Up Funds**
   Baptist General Convention of Texas—$8,000
   Union Baptist Association—$2,850
   Brentwood Baptist Church—$13,545
9. **Year Begun**
   1984
10. **Number of Pastors and Tenure**
   The Rev. M.E. Williams—4 years
   The Rev. Robert Dixon—4 years
11. **Method of Church Start**
   Church in transition

End Time Baptist Church

1. **Church Target Audience**
   Caribbean
2. **Location**
   Suburb: lower middle class, concentration of apartments
3. **Planter Profile**
   The Rev. Lewis Charles: Beaver Falls High School, Pennsylvania, 1962;
   Geneva College, Pennsylvania, BA
   Biblical Studies, 1974; BS Accounting
4. **Meeting Place History**
   1984-86—Brentwood Baptist Church Chapel
   1986-89—Day-care center
   1990-91—Pastor's home
   Present—Bought a three-bedroom house and converted it into a church

5. **Number of People Initially Involved**
   20
6. **Membership History**
   1st year—20
   2nd year—30
   3rd year—35, funding started in 1986
   4th year—57
   5th year—75
   6th year—new pastor, 1989
   7th year—90
   8th year—100
7. **Person(s) Responsible for Initiating Plant**
   Planter initiated
8. **Start-Up Funds**
   Baptist General Convention of Texas—$325
   Union Baptist Association—$100
   Brentwood Baptist Church—$400
   Utilized Brentwood Baptist Church chapel, free of
   charge, 2 years
9. **Year Begun**
   1984
10. **Number of Pastors and Tenure**
    The Rev. Lewis Charles—5 years
    The Rev. Matthew Ogbonmwan—6 months
11. **Method of Church Start**
    Core group/home Bible studies

St. Paul Baptist Church

1. **Church Target Audience**
   Middle class
2. **Location**
   Suburb: The Woodlands is a planned community.
   Homes start at $200,000+.

3. **Planter Profile**
   The Rev. Lewis James: Bivocational; married, two children; degree in technology, career in oil industry
4. **Meeting Place History**
   Started at Jimmy Dotson's home
   Interfaith center
5. **Number of People Initially Involved**
   12
6. **Membership History**
   1st year—56
   2nd year—85
   3rd year—80
   4th year—100
   5th year—175
   6th year—210
   7th year—350
7. **Person(s) Responsible for Initiating Plant**
   Union Baptist Association
8. **Start-Up Funds**
   Baptist General Convention of Texas—$400 monthly
   First Baptist Church, Woodlands—$500 monthly
   Brentwood Baptist Church—$500 monthly
   South Park Baptist Church—$100 monthly
   Tryon-Evergreen Baptist Association—$100 monthly
9. **Year Begun**
   1986
10. **Number of Pastors and Tenure**
    The Rev. Lewis James—1.5 years
    The Rev. George Ellis—3 months
    The Rev. James Harris—3 months
    The Rev. Lewis James—

11. **Method of Church Start**
    Special-event picnic which targeted all African-American families in this planned community

Greenspoint Baptist Church

1. **Church Target Audience**
   Middle class
2. **Location**
   Suburb: transitional neighborhood, median-priced homes
3. **Planter Profile**
   The Rev. Jimmy Wilson: college graduate; seminarian; wife and one son.
4. **Meeting Place History**
   Church facility in changing community
5. **Number of People Initially Involved**
   25
6. **Membership History**
   1st year—300
   2nd year—600
   3rd year—1,000
   4th year—1,200
   5th year—1,300
   6th year—1,300
   7th year—1,500
7. **Person(s) Responsible for Initiating Plant**
   Union Baptist Association
8. **Start-Up Funds**
   Baptist General Convention of Texas—$13,250
   Union Baptist Association—$1,650
   Brentwood Baptist Church—$26,968.55 (2 years @ $1,000 per month)

9. **Year Begun**
   1986

10. **Number of Pastors and Tenure**
   The Rev. Jimmy Wilson—four years
   Pulpit vacant April 1990-November 1991; the Rev.
   Menefee, formerly of Philadelphia, Pa., accepted
   pastorate.

11. **Method of Church Start**
   Anglo church in transition

Faith Baptist Church

1. **Church Target Audience**
   Middle class

2. **Location**
   Suburb: large concentration of condominiums and
   apartments.

3. **Planter Profile**
   The Rev. Alvin Molten: real estate broker; college
   graduate; married, 4 children.

4. **Meeting Place History**
   September 1987 rented facilities at Westbury Christian Church
   Hotel space—several months
   1988 to present: same facility

5. **Number of People Initially Involved**
   37

6. **Membership History**
   1st year—265
   2nd year—611
   3rd year—900
   4th year—1,110

7. **Person(s) Responsible for Initiating Plant**
   Planter initiated

8. **Start-Up Funds**
   Baptist General Convention of Texas—$7,900 from Sept. 1987-Dec. 1988
   Union Baptist Association—$2,150 from Sept. 1987-Dec. 1988
   Brentwood Baptist Church—$4,450 from Sept. 1987-Dec. 1988
9. **Year Begun**
   1987
10. **Number of Pastors and Tenure**
    The Rev. Alvin Molten—6 years
11. **Method of Church Start**
    Split

Bissonnet Baptist Church

1. **Church Target Audience**
   Middle class
2. **Location**
   Suburb: varied housing scheme—homes, condominiums and apartments
3. **Planter Profile**
   The Rev. Steve Crampton: Yates High School, Houston, 1972; University of Houston, 1972-75; Southwestern Baptist Theological Seminary; Youth Pastor-Holman St. Baptist, 1984-87, Houston, Texas; Pastor-St. Paul Baptist Church, 1987-89, Crockett, Texas
4. **Meeting Place History**
   Warehouse:
   1 space 1,250 sq. ft. for thirteen months
   2 spaces 3,600 sq. ft. for one month
   1 space of 1,250 sq. ft. at present

5. **Number of People Initially Involved**
   13
6. **Membership History**
   1st year—100
   2nd year—250
   3rd year—400
   4th year—600
7. **Person(s) Responsible for Initiating Plant**
   Planter initiated
8. **Start-Up Funds**
   Baptist General Convention of Texas—$500
   (3 months)
   Union Baptist Association—$200
   Brentwood Baptist Church—$750 (12 months)
   South Park Baptist Church—$200
   Start-up—$600
   One-time gift $7,500 Renovation
9. **Year Begun**
   September 1989
10. **Number of Pastors and Tenure**
    The Rev. Steve Crampton
11. **Method of Church Start**
    Home Bible studies

Heart of Houston Church

1. **Church Target Audience**
   Anglo upper and lower class
2. **Location**
   Inner city: gentrified luxury homes
3. **Planter Profile**
   The Rev. Doug Tipps: graduate of Baylor and
   Southwestern Baptist Theological Seminary; for-

merly pastor of River Oaks Baptist Church in Houston, Texas

4. **Meeting Place History**
   Grace Theater

5. **Number of People Initially Involved**
   13

6. **Membership History**
   1st year—50
   2nd year—150

7. **Person(s) Responsible for Initiating Plant**
   Planter initiated

8. **Start-Up Funds**
   Baptist General Convention of Texas—$2,400
   Union Baptist Association—$1,000
   Brentwood Baptist Church—6 months pastor insurance

9. **Year Begun**
   February 1991

10. **Number of Pastors and Tenure**
    The Rev. Doug Tipps

11. **Method of Church Start**
    Home Bible studies

Southwest Community Baptist Church

1. **Church Target Audience**
   Middle class

2. **Location**
   Suburb: homes start at $75,000+

3. **Planter Profile**
   The Rev. Gregg Patrick: Washington High School, 1970; Los Angeles, Calif.; Pepperdine University, BA, Journalism, 1974

4. **Meeting Place History**
   Printing shop at Southwest, at Community Church
5. **Number of People Initially Involved**
   19
6. **Membership History**
   1st year—97
   2nd year—210
   3rd year—300
7. **Person(s) Responsible for Initiating Plant**
   Planter initiated
8. **Start-Up Funds**
   Baptist General Convention of Texas—$800
   (4 months)
   Union Baptist Association—$200 (4 months)
9. **Year Begun**
   1991
10. **Number of Pastors and Tenure**
    The Rev. Gregg Patrick
11. **Method of Church Start**
    Home Bible studies
    Door-to-door

Faith Community Baptist Church

1. **Church Target Audience**
   Blue collar
2. **Location**
   Suburban: 10% Black population; 5,000 Black residents
3. **Planter Profile**
   The Rev. Michael Cox: B.A. Morehouse College, M.A. Religious Ed., Southwestern Theological Seminary; Associate Pastor, 1979-81; Research Assistant,

1980-81; Minister of Youth and Activities, 1981-82; Church Planter/Pastor, 1984-88

4. **Meeting Place History**
   July 1984—Afternoon worship in rented facilities of an American Baptist Church
   August 1984—Afternoon worship in sponsoring church facilities
   January 1985—Morning worship in elementary school
   April 1987—Morning worship in elementary school

5. **Number of People Initially Involved**
   7

6. **Membership History**
   1st year—100 resident members
   2nd year—150 resident members
   3rd year—230 resident members
   4th year—300 resident members

7. **Person(s) Responsible for Initiating Plant**
   2 sponsoring churches

8. **Start-Up Funds**
   Pastor's salary..$22,000
   Mission treasury $841
   Contributors:
   • Mt. Calvary Baptist Church (First Baptist, South Euclid)
   • Willoughby Baptist Church
   • State Convention of Baptists in Ohio
   • Home Mission Board

9. **Year Begun**
   1984

10. **Number of Pastors and Tenure**
    Michael Cox—4 years
    Phillip James—2 years

11. **Method of Church Start**
    Bible study/Special event worship

Bibliography

Barna, George. *The Frog in the Kettle.* California: Regal Books, 1990.

Dubois, William E.B., ed. *The Negro Church.* Atlanta University Report no. 8. 1903. Atlanta: Atlanta University Publications, II, 1903. Reprint. New York: Arno Press and *New York Times,* 1969.

Fauset, Arthur H. *Black Gods of the Metropolis.* 1944. Reprint. New York: Octagon Books, 1970.

Fitts, Leroy. *A History of Black Baptists.* Nashville: Broadman Press, 1985.

Frazier, E. Franklin. *The Negro Church in America.* New York: Schocken Books, 1963.

Gardiner, James A., and Deotis Roberts, eds. *Quest for a Black Theology.* Philadelphia: Pilgrim Press, 1971.

Jordon, Lewis G., *Negro Baptist History U.S.A. 1750-1930.* Nashville: Sunday School Publishing Board, National Baptist Convention, 1931.

Lewis, Larry L., *Organize to Evangelize.* Nashville: Broadman Press, 1988.

Mays, Benjamin E. , *The Negro's God.* New York: Chapman and Grimes, Inc., 1938.

Mays, Benjamin E. and John W. Nicholson. *The Negro's*

Church. New York: Institutes of Social and Religious Research, 1933.

McCall, Emmanuel L. *Black Church Lifestyles.* Nashville: Broadman Press, 1986.

Meier, August, and Elliott M. Rudwick. *From Plantation to Ghetto*. New York: Hill and Want, 1966.

Myrdal, Gunnar. *The Negro Social Structure*. Vol. 2 of *An American Dilemma*. New York: McGraw Hill Book Company, 1964.

Nelen, Hart M., Raytha L. Yokley, and Anne K. Nelsen, eds. *The Black Church in America*. New York: Basic Books, 1971.

Redford, Jack. *Planting New Churches*. Nashville: Broadman Press, 1978.

Reimers, David M. *White Protestantism and the Negro*. New York: Oxford University Press, 1965.

Schaller, Lyle E. *44 Questions for Church Planters*. Nashville: Abingdon Press, 1991.

Schaller, Lyle E. *It's a Different World*. Nashville: Abingdon Press, 1987.

Sernett, Milton C. *Black Religion and American Evangelicalism*. Metchuen, New Jersey: The Scarecrow Press, Incorporated, 1975.

Smith, Sid, compiler. *Church Planting*. Nashville: Convention Press, 1989.

Stuart, Karlton. *Black History and Achievement in America*. Arizona: Phoenix Books, 1982.

Washington, Joseph R., Jr., *Black Religion: The Negro and Christianity in the United States*. Boston: Beacon Press, 1966.

Wagner, C. Peter. *Church Planting for a Greater Harvest*. California: Regal, 1990.

Bibliography

Wilmore, Gayraud S. *Black Religion and Black Radicalism.* New York: Orbis Books, 1983.

Woodson, Carter G. *History of the Negro Church.* Washington, D.C.: The Associated Publishers, 1972.

About the Authors

Rev. Michael J. Cox is assistant director, Associational Missions Division, Mega Focus Cities Coordinator, Eastern Region, for the Home Mission Board, Southern Baptist Convention. Prior to coming to this position in 1992, Cox served for four years as associate director of the Black Church Extension Division of the Home Mission Board, Southern Baptist Convention. Former church planter and pastor of Faith Community Baptist Church in Euclid, Ohio, Rev. Cox received a Bachelor of Arts Degree from Morehouse College in Atlanta, Georgia, and a Master of Arts Degree from Southwestern Baptist Theological Seminary in Forth Worth, Texas.

Dr. Joe S. Ratliff is pastor of Brentwood Baptist Church in Houston, Texas, the largest black Southern Baptist church in America, and sponsor of seven mission churches in three years. Dr. Ratliff received a Bachelor of Arts Degree from Morehouse College in Atlanta, Georgia, and a Master of Divinity Degree and a Doctor of Ministry Degree from Interdenominational Theological Center in Atlanta, Georgia.